The Evil Twins of
American Television

The Evil Twins of American Television

Feminist Alter Egos since 1960

Kristi Rowan Humphreys

LEXINGTON BOOKS
Lanham • Boulder • New York • London

Published by Lexington Books
Lexington Books is an imprint of The Rowman & Littlefield Publishing Group, Inc.
4501 Forbes Boulevard, Suite 200, Lanham, Maryland 20706
www.rowman.com

6 Tinworth Street, London SE11 5AL, United Kingdom

British Library Cataloguing in Publication Information Available

Library of Congress Cataloging-in-Publication Data

ISBN 9781498583299 (cloth : alk. paper)
ISBN 9781498583305 (electronic)

♾™ The paper used in this publication meets the minimum requirements of American National Standard for Information Sciences—Permanence of Paper for Printed Library Materials, ANSI/NISO Z39.48-1992.

For my boys, Chris, Rowan, and Lawson

Contents

Figures

Acknowledgments

This book was supported by funds from the Baylor Arts & Humanities Faculty Research Program Committee and the Vice Provost for Research, and I am grateful. I would like to thank my institution, Baylor University, for giving me my dream job, the Chair of our English Department, Dr. Kevin Gardner, for always supporting my research and teaching interests, my students, for bringing me unimaginable joy every day, and Baylor's English Department—the best colleagues on earth—for making life so much fun.

Also, thanks to Karenna Malavanti, Mandy McMichael, Lauren Weber, and Nikki Glaros for their friendship, and to my family, Chris, Rowan, and Lawson, for loving me, even while enduring almost five years of evil-twin episodes on the family television.

Introduction

I was born the only child of three in my family to have dark hair and a large birth-mark on my temple. My older sister and younger brother—I am the *middle child*—both have beautiful blonde hair, and my dark hair color alone always made me feel different as a child. The birthmark on my face, though, sealed the deal in making me unique. Later, when I was the only one to develop freckles on my face, I thought I surely must have been adopted. My family was loving and encouraging and never did anything to make me feel "othered"; it just happened naturally because of my dark, curly hair, cloud-shaped birthmark, and freckles—three features neither of my siblings displayed.

Truth be told, I *was* different, and I spent much of my childhood jealous that my siblings' strengths weren't my strengths. They were always very good at things like . . . math and sports . . . and I had the incredibly marketable skill of headlining *The Kristi Show*, with my sidekick "Monkey-Laroo" (thanks, little brother), nightly on the hearth. These divisions continued throughout our adolescence. When my sister and I would play with our dolls, she would always get to be Barbie, and I had to be Skipper. I knew the rules—if you have dark hair, you have to be Skipper—but I always resisted playing by them. I'm proud to report that my sister and I have been able to resolve our Barbie/Skipper quarrels and grow to be best friends in adulthood, but in an effort to be fair to my parents, I should note that I was indeed their most challenging child. Simply put, I knew everything, and I never understood why it wasn't socially acceptable for me to remind people of that fact.

I begin with these personal details in an effort to create a framework for this study. As I have noted in my other projects, I grew up in the country as a child of the late seventies and early eighties, and we had three television channels, until Fox provided a fourth. Thus, we watched a great deal of movies on VHS tapes. Being so isolated, much of my identity came from the images communicated through television, but

1

that isn't uncommon. As Katharine Bullock rightly states, "Media ethnographers teach us that identity is partly related to issues of how our self and our community are represented in mass media. No matter the genre, be it news, sitcom, drama, thriller, or comedy, part of our involvement as viewers is to experience the program as it speaks to our sense of self."[1] I will never forget how much the film musical *Annie* resonated with me as a child because I saw a feisty, curly-headed, freckle-faced girl become whatever she wanted. After watching the movie a mere eight hundred times, I remember deciding that I would be Annie. (Still to this day, I have insisted that I would name my first daughter Annie. Alas, I have all sons.) I also watched reruns of *Bewitched*, *I Dream of Jeannie*, and *The Patty Duke Show* religiously as a child, and whereas a part of me wanted to be offended that these shows always made the evil twins have dark hair and beauty marks like me (the jury is still out, though, on whether my birthmark can be associated in any way with "beauty"), I couldn't be offended because I saw too much of myself in those twins. They were me, and I was them—the Skipper to the family's Barbie. I wanted to travel the world, fly helicopters, enter kite-flying championships, run for office—all activities performed by the evil twins of these shows. To the adolescent me, the message was clear: it is okay for me to pursue these things as a child (like Annie), but by the time I become an adult, I'd better transition from the Serena of my heart to the Samantha of my head. As a side note, the alignment of the evil twins with childish behavior is not my observation alone; in one of the female-written *Bewitched* episodes, "Tabitha's Very Own Samantha," Samantha says explicitly of evil cousin Serena, "Don't worry about her. She's like a child. Her attention span is highly limited."[2] Furthermore, the childlike, evil-twin antics, in addition to the magic and special effects, may have also been a reason that, in addition to adults, children like me were so drawn to these shows and characters.[3]

These adolescent observations are how this project began, as I carried my affectionate memories of *Bewitched*, *The Patty Duke Show*, and *I Dream of Jeannie* into graduate school, a college teaching career, and my research, which is why so much of my scholarship has focused on television of this era. In fact, my very first publication was a chapter titled "Supernatural Housework: Magic and Domesticity in 1960s Television." I have always respected the work of Susan J. Douglas, namely, *Where the Girls Are: Growing Up Female with the Mass Media*, and I found myself wanting to respond to some of her observations. Douglas argues that several of these shows of the 1960s depict both the growth of and public unease with the women's liberation movement, but that when characters like Jeannie or Samantha claim to be subordinate, while actually possessing the powers to dominate, they are implying to the audience "that male authority wasn't so impregnable or impressive at all."[4] This valid observation didn't completely align with my own interpretations of these series, so my "Supernatural" chapter argues that while "popular interpretations of the supernatural qualities of 1960s television tend to view them as representations of the emerging female sexual and political energy of the decade, through 'supernatural housework,' the sixties characters of Samantha Stephens (*Bewitched*), Jeannie (*I*

Dream of Jeannie), and Morticia Addams (*The Addams Family*) actually furthered the dominant gender discourse of the fifties—one which suggested that fulfillment for women had only one definition: housewifery."[5] Later, I extended this research in my monograph, *Housework and Gender in American Television: Coming Clean*, where I argue that when representations of housework are viewed as maternal practice—the act of preservation—strength is inherent in the activity of service.

Through all of this, though, I haven't been able to get the evil twins of 1960s television off of my mind, and my education and adult experiences have only caused me to think more deeply about their impact. Thus, in an effort to identify how these artifacts engage their social contexts—the ultimate goal of all of my related publications—my analysis of the evil twins of 1960s television leads me to make a twofold argument. First, I argue that the good/evil twins are representations of what Betty Friedan called the "schizophrenic split" (which I will subsequently call the "split") in her seminal work, *The Feminine Mystique*—representations that served to place these shows in conversation with Friedan and the 1960s feminist dialogue. The evil twins are depicted as embodying the characteristics of the evil side of Friedan's split and of seeking to perform and succeed in the male-dominated public sphere, while the good twins find contentment in their proper roles, dominating the private sphere. Second, I argue that they functioned in tandem with the happy housewife characters to *create* the housewife consumer in reality. As I've stated elsewhere, "real American women were watching and learning from these characters. In fact, the American homemaker—the person deemed responsible for buying her household products— was the primary target of television advertisers around this time.[6] But advertising and production executives were not just seeking to appeal to the American homemaker."[7] In her seminal work *Living Room Lectures: The Fifties Family in Film and Television*, Nina C. Leibman argued that, through the presentation of a particular version of femininity in relation to domesticity, these executives were seeking to show her what she ought to be—to "*create*" her."[8] Here, I take this argument a step further by claiming that the evil twins functioned to support this goal. By also showing the American woman what she ought *not* to be, these shows were able to use the two depictions together to more effectively program women as America's consumers.

PANDORA'S BOX AND THE FEMME FATALE

The "evil woman" trope has a well-established history, dating back to the Greek myth of Pandora's box—a myth that serves to connect 1960s television to Greek mythology. In this mythological story, Zeus (Olympian god) seeks to punish Prometheus (Titan) for stealing the element of fire from the gods and giving it to humankind, so Zeus has Prometheus chained to the side of a cliff. Zeus then decides to punish humankind for accepting the gift of fire from Prometheus, and he demands that a woman be created—a woman that is so beautiful she will be irresistible to gods and men. Zeus names her Pandora and has all of the other gods and goddesses bestow gifts upon her. Hera gives her the gift of curiosity, which will ultimately lead to her downfall. Pandora is sent down to earth with a gilded box and is told that she should never open the box. Every time Pandora looks at the box, however, she wants to open it. Finally, one day her curiosity gets the best of her and she opens the box. Using the key that hangs around her neck, she unlocks it, opens the box, and consequently releases all of the evil and wickedness upon the earth—evil that Zeus had locked away in the box to plague humankind. Rather than be content with what she had been given, Pandora succumbs to her curiosity—a curiosity that ultimately leads to evil. Thus, just as the story of Adam and Eve implies, curiosity (namely, in women), rather than unquestionable contentment, leads to evil.

This myth's influence on the sixties televised evil-twin narrative is fairly obvious, considering the decade's most popular show, *Bewitched*, references the myth explicitly. In the beginning of the series, Elizabeth Montgomery is credited with portraying both roles of Samantha Stephens and her identical cousin, Serena. After about a dozen of the Serena episodes, though, the show decides to publish a different name for the actress playing Serena, selecting the name "Pandora Spocks," an obvious reference to the Pandora's box myth. Just as the myth of Pandora is credited with unleashing the world's evil upon humankind, Serena unleashes her own brand of evil on the entire series.

Much later, the "evil woman" theme is adopted by the "femme fatale" trope of the cinema—a trope that serves to connect the evil in women with feminism, production, and representation. In American cinema, the femme fatale dates back to the silent era, but film noir is the genre that enjoys the most active development of the trope and provides some of the richest examples of women using sexuality and intellect to lure men. In her book *Femmes Fatales: Feminism, Film Theory, Psychoanalysis*, Mary Ann Doane describes how the "femme fatale" functioned to highlight anxieties regarding shifts in the "understanding of sexual difference" in the 19th century: ". . . it is appropriate that the femme fatale is represented as the antithesis of the maternal—sterile or barren, she produces nothing in society which fetishizes production . . . the femme fatale is situated as evil and is frequently punished or killed . . . She is not the subject of feminism but a symptom of male fears about feminism."[9] Some of the most famous examples of the "femme fatale" in American cinema include the character Phyllis Dietrichson (played by Barbara Stanwick) in *Double Indemnity*,[10] Norma Desmond (Gloria Swanson) in *Sunset Boulevard*,[11] and Madeleine Elster (Kim Novak) in *Vertigo*.[12] Thus, Greek mythology, female representations in various art forms, and developments of the "femme fatale" trope all serve to pave the way in popular culture for mid-century representations of women—representations that were at the fore of Betty Friedan's observations in the sixties.

THE FEMININE MYSTIQUE AND TELEVISION

When Friedan wrote *The Feminine Mystique* in 1963, she identified something she called "the problem that has no name"—the voice stirring inside housewives of the era that said, "I want something more than my husband and children and home."[13] She claimed the women most afflicted by this "problem" were not career women, but the ones whose greatest ambition in life involved marriage and children alone.[14] Just as Victorian women supposedly buried their need for sex, mid-century housewives suppressed a need, a desire to do more than they were doing—to do and be something they could not necessarily articulate.[15] This stirring was "not a matter of loss of femininity or too much education, or the demands of domesticity," or even sex; according to Friedan, the voice housewives suppress—the desire for something beyond housewifery—involved much more than this. It seemed, in part, to be somehow connected to a longing to be someone who does not exist solely in and through others. It seemed to be connected on some level to self-service—something often ascribed to the career—instead of exclusively self-sacrifice—a quality often associated with housewifery.

From this perspective, the image of the American woman is split in two, forming multiple strict oppositional binaries—housewife versus career woman, good versus evil, self versus other, private versus public.[16] Friedan connected this mid-century split to past images that celebrated the pure, virgin woman and condemned the sexual, desirous one:

> The split in the new image opens a different fissure—the feminine woman, whose goodness includes the desires of the flesh, and the career woman, whose evil includes every desire of the separate self. The new feminine morality story is the exorcising of the forbidden career dream, the heroine's victory over Mephistopheles: the devil, first in the form of a career woman, who threatens to take away the heroine's husband or child, and finally, the devil inside the heroine herself, the dream of independence, the discontent of spirit, and even the feeling of a separate identity that must be exorcised to win or keep the love of husband and child.[17]

It is especially significant that Friedan associates one side of the split with evil specifically, equating career, independence, discontent, and the need for separate identity with the "devil inside." In other words, the impediments keeping women from realizing their full potential now involved something more than the lack of opportunities, equality, and resources, in part conquered by the feminisms of the past. According to Friedan, "the only problems now are those that might disturb her adjustment as a housewife. So career is a problem, education is a problem, political interest, even the very admission of women's intelligence and individuality is a problem."[18] The implication here is twofold: first, women will happily remain in the home if their adjustment to housewifery is successfully facilitated, and two, this adjustment is dependent upon regarding career, independence, and political interest as evil forces. The split indicates that women had only two choices. When presented with these two options, many women, some highly educated, preferred the safer option of housewifery, using their many years of education to change sheets, attend PTA meetings, and bathe children. This is not to say these activities are not fulfilling, valuable, and reflective of a desire to preserve; surely, these women showed a great deal of strength in committing to a life a service.[19] The point here is that, even though Friedan claims that "real women embody the split in the image,"[20] women still felt they must choose between the strict oppositional constructs reflected in the new image of woman created by American popular culture—a culture within which television played a significant role.

With regard to representations of gender and family in mid-century television, Leibman claimed that television content adhered "to a strict oppositional construct in which men and boys are associated ideally with strength, intelligence, logic, consistency, and humor, while women and girls are rendered intuitive, dependent, flighty, sentimental, and self-sacrificing."[21] More to the point of this study, she states the following: "By the same token, characters who shun these traits, or who adopt those belonging to the opposite sex, are deemed dysfunctional (if they are men) or evil (if they are women). Such adopted traits include, for men, domesticity, refinement, and emotionality, and for women, ambition, assertiveness, and independence."[22]

Similar to Friedan's equation (evil equals career, political interest, and separate self, for example), Leibman adds assertiveness to the list of qualities reflective of the "devil inside," of the evil side of the split American woman image. That said, American popular culture's message was clear: a woman can either commit happily to self-sacrifice, service, self-effacement, and housewifery (by suppressing the "voice"), and enjoy the concomitant rewards of goodness, security, and admiration, or a woman can entertain the "devil inside" through career, independence, political interest, and assertiveness (by indulging the "voice"), and suffer the consequences of evil, uncertainty, and degradation.

Friedan directly addresses television and its lack of female leads in her essay, "Television and the Feminine Mystique":

> Why for instance, isn't one of the leads in a program like *Mr. Novak* [a show about a high-school English teacher] a woman teacher? I asked MGM executive producer Norman Felton. He explained: "If you have a woman lead in a television series, she has to be either married or unmarried. If she's unmarried, what's wrong with her? After all, it's housewives we're appealing to, and marriage is their whole life. If she's married, what's her husband doing in the background? He must not be very effective. He should be making the decisions. For drama, there has to be action, conflict. If the action is led by a woman, she has to be in conflict—with men or women or something. She has to

make decisions; she has to triumph over opposition. For a woman to make decisions, to triumph over anything, would be unpleasant, dominant, masculine. After all, most women are housewives, at home with children; most women are dominated by men, and they would react against a woman who succeeded at anything."[23]

Felton's explanation is directly related to the function of the evil alter egos, who are perceived as evil by the other characters because they do all of the things—make decisions, triumph over opposition—Felton identifies as being "unpleasant, dominant, masculine." Friedan's ultimate assessment is that 1960s television depicted woman as "a stupid, unattractive, insecure little household drudge . . ." In his book, *Bewitched*, Walter Metz finds that "Samantha on *Bewitched* represented an antidote to the kind of women Friedan lamented about being on American television; in fact, Endora uses Friedan's exact words, such as 'drudge' and 'boring,' to describe Sam's life with Darrin."[24] *I Dream of Jeannie* does the same, when Jeannie is depicted as reading a women's magazine article about being a modern women—an article that instructs on "How not to be a drudge."[25] I agree that characters like Samantha and Jeannie represent antidotes to Friedan's observations; the shows featured female leads who had powers the men do not have. But these characters also swear off their powers to please their men. In other words, characters have the ability to perform in the public sphere while never leaving the private sphere—a terrifying prospect for the shows' men, who constantly express their disapproval. The Samanthas and Jeannies of these shows are typically apologetic for having and using power, but the alter egos unapologetically own their abilities to perform in the public sphere. In fact, Metz finds that Serena—and I argue, all of the alter egos—"represents traditional feminism unfettered by the patriarchal imperatives of 1960s traditional feminism."[26] So whereas these shows provided images of housewives that didn't appear boring, answering Friedan's call to action, they also presented non-housewives (the evil twins) as countercultural.

THE 1960S, VISUAL CULTURE, AND THE TWINNING TROPE

As the decade of the civil rights movement, the Vietnam War, and second-wave feminism, the 1960s experienced immense change and unrest. In all of these shows, the cultural climate made its way into the living room—or onto the island, in the case of *Gilligan's Island*. Consequently, Metz argues that these shows should be regarded as an important "collection of cultural historical documents that uncompromisingly negotiate the political climate surrounding it."[27] What is perhaps most notable about this decade, though, is its culture versus counterculture, or as television scholars Lynn Spigel and Michael Curtin call it, "us vs. them" logic.[28] Following a period of intense postwar conformity, the 1960s witnessed the emergence of "types" who did not fit with mainstream society, and various binary oppositions—where one was either this or that, at the extremes of either normal or deviant—often define the culture of the decade. For women and television representations thereof, this often meant navigating the oppositions between social demands and personal preference.

Prior to the 1960s and the popularity of television, though, visual culture had an established history of dealing with these oppositions through the trope of twinning, but even though examples exist of the twinning trope being applied to male charac-ters—examples include *Star Trek*, when Captain Kirk and Spock meet evil Kirk and Spock, and *Bonanza*, when Little Joe meets his evil twin, an escaped prisoner—such examples are vastly lower in number compared to twin examples involving women. For example, the 1946 film *The Dark Mirror*[29] presents a plot centered on identical female twins Ruth and Terry Collins (both played by Olivia de Havilland), a murder, and a psychiatrist, Dr. Scott Elliott (Lew Ayres), who is a "twin expert." One of the twins has been seen leaving the apartment of a murdered man, but when both twins claim to have alibis, no one is able to identify which twin was at the scene of the crime. As with the television examples analyzed in this study, one twin is depicted as good (Ruth) and the other as evil (Terry). After studying the twins for months, the doctor comes to the conclusion that "Terry is sick inside, twisted inside," and he falls for the innocent and proper Ruth. Through the doctor's dialogue, the film supports these oppositional binaries in depictions of women by claiming that "all women are rivals fundamentally," "there is a natural strong rivalry between sisters," and identical twins, especially, deal with the "agonies of jealousy." Most telling, per-haps, is when the doctor concludes in the end, "That's what twins are: reflections of each other—everything in reverse." Twinning seemed to be the perfect mechanism to communicate the ways in which women were regarded as being "this" or "that."

This idea has been furthered in several films, including the 1946 film, *A Stolen Life*,[30] which stars Bette Davis playing twin sisters Kate and Patricia Bosworth. As with common uses of the twinning trope, Kate is depicted as being proper, loyal, creative, and good-natured, while Patricia is depicted as being a jealous and conniv-ing woman who smokes and drinks. When Patricia drowns in a boating accident, Kate assumes her identity in order to be with Patricia's husband, with whom Kate fell in love before Patricia began dating him. Later, in 1961, the popular film *The Parent Trap* (remade in 1998 with Lindsey Lohan in the lead role) starred Hailey Mills in both roles as twin sisters, Susan Evers and Sharon McKendrick, separated at birth. The film was based on a 1949 novel, *Lottie and Lisa*, by Erich Kastner. In 1964, Bette Davis made a film similar to her previous 1949 work titled *Dead Ringer*,[31] which, like most other examples, featured identical twin sisters—one be-ing a good "type" and the other an evil one—and assumed identities. And finally, in 1971, *Twins of Evil*[32] presented identical twins Maria and Frieda Gellhorn (Mary and Madeline Collinson). Frieda gets into trouble because she is not content with her new life, while Maria remains pure and devoted.

Television of the 1960s picked up the practice of reflecting "types" explicitly by drawing on this established trope of "twinning," as the decade included a pervasive use of evil doppelgängers for both men and women as a way of dealing with this "us vs. them" logic. In his work *Comic Visions*, David Marc discusses this trend of twinning, claiming it "is typical of the sitcom's treatment of 'counterculture types' during the sixties."[33] For the 1960s, twinning was clearly television's well-known convention for depicting the "other"—the individuals in society who are not a part of the common "acceptable" culture. Considering the 1960s is often defined by this "us vs. them" logic, it is no surprise that the doubling/twinning trope was so popular in television of this decade. While popular, though, 1960s examples of female evil twins vastly outnumber examples of male evil twins; furthermore, episodes that include male twins received very different treatments. For example, in the *Bonanza* episode "Mirror of a Man" (1963),[34] Jud Lolly, wearing light tan clothes and a red bandana around his neck, meets his evil twin Rube, who wears dark clothes from head to toe (both characters played by Ron Hayes). Jud comes from a family of convicts (the Barnes) but has chosen to change his name from Homer Barnes to Jud Lolly in an effort to marry well and lead a more honest life. His twin brother, Rube, and their father "Pa" (Ford Rainey) are still living lives of crime. In this episode, Rube kills a man to steal a horse. When Jud finds out, he brings food and supplies to help Rube and his father while they are in hiding, and Jud insists they return the horse. When Rube finds out that Jud has saved $150 with his wife, Amelia (Nancy Rennick), to buy a house, Rube makes a plan to get the money, saying, "The only difference between Homer and me is he is clean and his belly is full, while I am dirty and my belly is empty. She (Amelia) will fix one, and the other don't show." Rube decides to switch places with Jud, while their father holds Jud at gunpoint, in order to get to the money and run away. In another example, the *Star Trek* episode "Mirror, Mirror" (1967)[35,36] depicts the Enterprise crew encountering some of their evil counterparts, including an evil Spock with a goatee (both roles played by Leonard Nimoy) and an evil Sulu with a large scar on his right cheek (both roles played by George Takei), in a parallel universe. Evil Spock almost kills a crew member for not being successful in implementing his orders, and evil Sulu threatens to kill in an effort to be promoted. Once the good Enterprise crew is returned to their proper universe, Captain Kirk (William Shatner) asks the good Spock how he was able to identify the evil doppelgängers so quickly. Spock responds, "It was far easier for you, as civilized men, to pretend to behave like barbarians than it was for them, as barbarians, to behave like civilized men." Even *Gilligan's Island* used the twinning trope with both male and female characters, and the treatment of each is very different. For example, in "Gilligan vs. Gilligan," a Soviet spy arrives on the island, looking exactly like Gilligan (Bob Denver) and planning to assume his identity to spy on the others. Once the spy has learned Gilligan's dialect and mannerisms, he is told by his superiors to "get rid of him [the real Gilligan]." The spy pulls out his gold pocket knife and goes to find and attempt to kill Gilligan. The spy is unable to use the knife, so he slams a rock into Gilligan's head, with the plans of killing him. Gilligan is merely knocked unconscious, though, so the spy ties and gags him and assumes his identity. The episode's social commentary of including a Soviet spy is discussed further in chapter 4.

These examples of male evil-twin depictions in the 1960s are significant because they differ drastically from female evil-twin depictions. As these examples reveal, when male characters have evil twins, the twin is considered a barbarian, a criminal, a murderer—a person who seems to display actual "evil." Even when these male evil twins are given second chances, they still desire to behave badly, leading one to believe there is something inherently evil about them. Before discussing how the female twins are depicted very differently, I must note one female evil-twin episode from the 1960s that receives more of the aforementioned male-twin treatment than the female; the complicated alter ego in this example is not only evil (with domestic affinities and talents) but is intentionally designed to be evil *through* domestic affinities and talents—which is why I am mentioning it here instead of in the lengthier analysis sections. In the fifth season of *Get Smart* (1965–1971), the episode "And Only Two Ninety-Nine"[37] applies the twinning trope to the character Ninety-Nine. Written by Arne Sultan and directed by Don Adams, the episode opens with Ninety-Nine reading a June *Bride* magazine. Automatically, the show aligns this character, whomever she may be, with the good side of the split, as she is diligently devoting time to planning a wedding. She has a black eye, though, so she doesn't fit the mold precisely, and Max asks about it. She claims, "I was leaning over to pick up some diapers, and I hit it on the bassinette." Her answer to an often-masculine problem in these situations on television—a black eye—involves a domestic—typically female— answer. Max asks how her day with her mother went. Ninety-Nine tells him she canceled, and Max indicates that that isn't like her because he knows how much she enjoys spending the day with her mother. Ninety-Nine explains that she just had too much to do. That evening, she goes to sleep, and the phone rings twice but doesn't wake her. Max answers. The chief is calling, saying, "That woman in the other bed is not Ninety-Nine." The episode establishes later that the woman is a Russian spy named Sonya.

In the next scene, the real Ninety-Nine is observing this and humorously responds, "Well, I'm certainly glad I put on clean sheets this morning," which again indicates that when dealing with the competition of another woman, television writers use examples of domesticity as the defense. Ninety-Nine explains the situation, saying, "I had just put the twins to bed. I went downstairs and heard the doorbell ring." There, she finds her evil twin, who is wearing dark blue, while she is wearing bright orange. The proceeding scenes pit one woman's domestic abilities against the other, which is one reason the episode doesn't follow the formula this study claims as an industry standard. Also, though, the alter ego is actually evil, as she has been programmed to kill Max, which differs from the other female alter egos, who are depicted as merely desiring a sense of independence, rather than to commit crimes of theft or murder.

Next morning, Max only wants coffee and toast for breakfast. Sonya made a full breakfast that he doesn't want to eat. He refuses, so she seduces him, sitting in his lap, kissing his neck and ears. Eventually, Max claims, "Fake Ninety-Nine is doing a lot of things real Ninety-Nine wouldn't do. She sat on my lap and fed me breakfast and kissed me so passionately on my way out that I didn't want to go to work. Real Ninety-Nine just gives me a peck." In this way, the episode does follow the trends established by the other female evil-twin episodes: the female evil twin is always more sexual than the good twin. The twist, here, is that her appeal is also combined with her domesticity. The chief tells Max that he has to make her believe that he believes she is the real Ninety-Nine. Indicating his attraction to the evil twin's unique combination of sexual desire and superior domestic abilities, Max replies, "Chief, if I have to spend more than a week with this woman, I am willing to do it. And if I have to spend two weeks with this woman, I'm willing to do it." In the end, Sonya tries to use her cooking and baking skills to poison Max over time and kill him, but Ninety-Nine arrives, punches Sonya (in another masculine move), and saves the day. The depictions in this episode seem to align more with typical uses of the twinning trope with male characters versus female characters, but this remains from my research the sole example that follows the male-twin pattern.

Female evil twins are depicted very differently from these examples in 1960s television. They do not desire to murder or break the law. Their evil involves attributes identified by Friedan: having loose inhibitions, career interests, political interests, or intellectual prowess, and, in general, being too assertive. Addressing the *Bewitched* evil cousin, Serena, specifically, Marc claims evil alter-ego characters like this were "portrayed as silly and impractical, rather than malevolent or evil." However, since I argue that Friedan's split is explicitly manifest through the plot and character device of "twinning," the actions and dialogue appropriately perceived by Marc as "silly and impractical" are forced to belong to the evil side of the split, when American popular culture was demanding one must fall on one side or the other of the strict oppositional binary it had created for women.[38] Furthermore, using Marc's locution, the depiction of these twins as "silly and impractical" would align them with the 1960s mainstream perception, according to historian William L. O'Neill, of feminism: "One of the peculiarities of modern history is that feminism is always thought ridiculous."[39] Just as sections of mainstream society saw feminism as ridiculous, these female alter egos, who often embody feminist ideals, were depicted as silly, impractical, and in a post–*Feminine Mystique* society, evil.

In addition to the twinning trope, though, these series have a lot in common. First, not all of these shows were popular with critics in their time. For example, even though *I Dream of Jeannie*, *Gilligan's Island*, and *The Brady Bunch* have devoted followings now, they were not industry favorites when they initially aired. Furthermore, there are similarities in the functions of their narratives. In his chapter, "The Unworthy Discourse: Situation Comedy in Television," Paul Attallah notes the following about sitcom narratives such as these: "It is a narrative necessity of situation comedy that the 'situation' must remain unchanged. If the program is to be repeated week after week, the characters and their mode of interaction must not be allowed to evolve. Were they to acquire experience, then evolution would occur and the show would not continue."[40] Just as the castaways on *Gilligan's Island* can't manage to steal Eva's boat in the evil-twin episode "All About Eva" and Jeannie can grant Tony's wishes, even though he continues to get into trouble in many scenes of *I Dream of Jeannie*, episode after episode, the comedy of these shows relies upon the unchanged nature of their situations.

SYDNEY SHELDON, PATTY DUKE,
AND *THE FEMININE MYSTIQUE*

One of the first very popular shows to use twinning to depict "types" in 1960s television involved the identical cousins, Patty and Cathy Lane (both played by Patty Duke), in *The Patty Duke Show*—a show that Nielsen ratings placed in the top thirty for multiple seasons. In her chapter "Girl Watchers: Patty Duke and Teen TV," Moya Luckett argues that "*The Patty Duke Show* dealt with these problems by centering the narrative around a doubling, a *disruption* of identity, thus representing the difficulty, unpredictability, and protean nature of teenage behavior."[41] Additionally, though, this doubling also represents the split Friedan identified upon publication of *The Feminine Mystique* in February of 1963; *The Patty Duke* show began airing in September of that same year, making the book's influence on the series possible if not probable.

In the unaired pilot, Patty and Cathy are presented as identical cousins, the daughters of fathers who are twin brothers. As the lyrics of the opening tune indicate, these cousins are "one pair of matching bookends, different as night and day: Cathy adores a minuet, the Ballet Russes, and Crepe Suzettes. Patty loves to rock and roll, a hot dog makes her lose control. What a wild duet." Cathy is depicted as being obedient, polite, and thoughtful, while Patty dislikes things like housework and homework and concocts crazy schemes to get what she wants. Whereas Luckett's argument regarding these depictions as "representing the difficulty, unpredictability, and protean nature of teenage behavior" is certainly valid, these portrayals also support Friedan's conclusion that the image of the American woman is split in two. Since *The Patty Duke Show* played such an important role in in the popularity of the twinning trope in sixties television and seems to have a strong connection to the "split" issues Friedan identified, it is worth examining the life, work, and words of the show's creator, Sydney Sheldon, whose influence is tied to a majority of the shows and episodes—including *The Patty Duke Show, Bewitched,* and *I Dream of Jeannie*—analyzed in this study. Consequently, even though it is difficult in television studies to use the term "author" or even *auteur*, because television series are considered corporate products, with the influences of many, from producers and directors to actors and designers, going into the making of every episode, I will do so when it comes to the productions of Sheldon. His influence on his programs was just that significant—something I will discuss further in the methodology section.

In 2005, Sheldon published his autobiography, *The Other Side of Me*, which detailed his life as a film, television, stage, and eventually, novel writer and his early struggles with suicide and the eventual diagnosis of bipolar disorder, a condition that likely inspired the title of his memoir. This work is especially telling because of how it connects Sheldon with the "split identity" issues found in *The Feminine Mystique*. First, Sheldon describes his one date with Marilyn Monroe around 1956: "She began to talk. To my surprise, the thrust of the conversation was Dostoyevsky, Pushkin, and several other Russian writers. What she was saying seemed so incongruous coming from this beautiful young woman, that it was as though I were having dinner with two different people. I felt she had no real grasp of what she was talking about."[42] Even though this outing with Monroe precedes the publication of *The Feminine Mystique*, Sheldon's recounting of the event does not. This passage indicates that Sheldon was at least thinking about the split identities of women at the time: Monroe's knowledge of writers was incongruous with Sheldon's idea of a sex symbol. In

Figure 0.1. Patty Duke in *The Patty Duke Show*, Archive PL / Alamy Stock Photo

other words, to Sheldon, they should be two different people—a beautiful woman *or* a well-read, intelligent one.

Furthermore, many of Sheldon's earliest episodes of *The Patty Duke Show* reveal telling views on housework and the roles of women. First, in the unaired pilot, the Lane family has a housekeeper—something that changes in all subsequent episodes. When Cathy arrives from Scotland, she heads to Martin's work at the *San Francisco Express*. Martin's boss thinks Cathy is Patty and asks about the location of her father. When she says he is in Scotland, the boss impulsively assumes Martin has quit; consequently, he gives Martin's job to someone else. Once the family hears the news that Martin has lost his job, they begin thinking of ways to cut back on expenses. Mrs. Lane is the first to respond, saying, "I love doing my own housework. It keeps me slim." Sheldon's dialogue corresponds directly with ideas presented in *The Feminine Mystique*. Friedan claims that "The True Housewife" and the "Balanced Homemaker" are depicted as preferring "to have sufficient appliances and do the housework themselves" versus the "Career Woman," who is depicted as preferring servants because "housework takes too much time and energy."[43] Another early *Patty Duke Show* episode, "The Birds and the Bees Bit,"[44] furthers these sentiments. In this episode, Ross is having "girl troubles," so he seeks advice from his father. Martin says, "As you get older, Ross, you'll develop more mature interests, and girls will be one of them." Ross responds, "Not me. I'm never going to get married. You have to support your wife for the rest of your life, and what does she do for you?" Martin answers, "Oh, she'll cook, clean, be a companion, nurse you when you're sick, wash the dishes, do the laundry, bring up your children." Ross's perspective is understandable and humorous for his age, but Martin's response is revealing in terms of Sheldon's views regarding the function of women and television's influence on gender roles.

Moreover, one of the most revealing episodes, regarding Sheldon's awareness of the main points of Friedan's work, is "Are Mothers People?"[45] This episode, also written by Sheldon, addresses not only some of the housewife issues raised by Friedan but also the dark-haired, sultry evil-woman stereotype (through the character of Joan). The episode opens with Natalie preparing four different breakfasts for her family, while the family members call out from the dining room, "When is breakfast going to be ready?" Natalie turns on her kitchen radio and listens to a female psychologist discussing the lives of housewives, saying, "One of the major problems of the modern housewife is that she is taken for granted. She is no more than a useful piece of furniture around the house, and she is treated as such." Natalie tells the radio doctor that "she has a lot to learn." When she delivers the four breakfasts to her family, no one thanks her or even notices her; instead, they make various demands of her for the day, from sewing buttons to making phone calls. Once they leave, she asks her friend Joan to come over. Joan has dark, black hair (like all of the evil twins studied herein), wears fur (a costume choice that, in other series like *Bewitched*, functions to align the evil twins with being hunters, rather than prey), wears more than average makeup and jewelry, and speaks in a sultry tone. Natalie tells her that when that radio psychologist mentioned what a big problem the lack of appreciation is to the modern housewife (i.e., part of Friedan's "problem that has no name"), she realizes it is true in her experience, as well. Natalie asks Joan if she thinks she is making a "mountain out of a mole hill." Joan says "no" and tells her that it is time the mothers of the world unite and form a union (i.e., the evil friend Joan attempts to transfer her political interests to Natalie). She convinces Natalie to lie (i.e., the evil friend encourages loose inhibitions) to her family in various ways, such as pretending to be sick so that they will miss and appreciate her. When that lie fails, Joan convinces Natalie to pay attention only to herself all day (i.e., the evil friend teaches selfishness) by taking a spa day and buying a new dress and jewelry. The family still does not notice Natalie, and Martin even tells her she should organize her time better, saying, "If businessmen ran their businesses as haphazardly as the average home is run, nothing would ever get done" (i.e., the husband criticizes the career potential of a woman).[46] According to Joan, the third step involves Natalie staying out late that night at dinner with Joan, without telling the family where she is, so as to make them worry about her. Over tea, Natalie tells Joan that she feels guilty because she didn't even fix them dinner. Joan tells her to stop thinking of them and to start thinking about herself. Natalie asks, "How can I? They *are* me" (i.e., Friedan asserted that women were expected to define themselves by their roles as wives and mothers). When Natalie says she thinks she should go home, Joan responds, "Alright, if you want to be an unappreciated household *drudge* for the rest of your life" (i.e., this reiterates Friedan's claim regarding the "drudgery" of the housewife's existence). The episode ends with the family showing Natalie their appreciation, but this example reflects Friedan's influence throughout, particularly by including the "invisible" work of housewives, the insistence that women define themselves by wife and mother roles, and the "drudgery" of housework.

Returning to Sheldon's autobiography, in a 2000 interview conducted by Henry Colman for The Television Academy Foundation, Sheldon describes how he came up with the basic premise for *The Patty Duke Show*, claiming that the network approached him with a show title, a lead actress, and a time slot but with no idea for a show. After spending time with Patty Duke (whose real name is Anna) and seeing her work as Helen Keller in the 1962 film *The Miracle Worker*, Sheldon decided that she was so talented, "she could do two parts, [because] one part wouldn't capture it all."[47] Duke tells a similar story in her interview with Stephen J. Abramson for The Television Academy Foundation: "Sydney decided that he wanted both sides of my personality to be represented, and that's how he invented identical cousins."[48] (Incidentally, Sheldon admits that his first concept for the show involved Patty and Cathy as twin sisters, but the idea to make them identical cousins came from William Asher, who would later direct several *Patty Duke* episodes and *Bewitched*—a show that also utilized the good/evil-twin trope extensively.) In the same interview, Duke opens up about her dual role, split personas, and bipolar disorder. When asked whether she enjoyed playing the role of Cathy more than Patty, Duke responds, "Yes, because I liked the earnestness of her [Cathy]. She seemed more mature. Cathy was my favorite because she was calm and sedate and spoke nicely. I didn't like Patty. She embarrassed me." Then, when asked if these two characters potentially represented two sides of her to some degree, Duke replied, "Oh, yeah. He [Sheldon] nailed it, absolutely nailed it on the head. Who knew that he was prescient, and I would eventually be diagnosed bipolar?" Finally, when asked how she approached both of the roles, Duke said, "They were not going to be two whole people. In order to create one, I had to take away from the other . . . Bill Asher [William Asher, the director] was incredibly helpful."[49] These statements are significant because *The Patty Duke Show* is the earliest example analyzed in this study. Because of the show's popularity, it is also likely that subsequent examples were influenced by it and its creators/participants. Thus, the combined efforts and viewpoints of Duke, Sheldon, and Asher influenced characters and plots that helped to construct Friedan's assessment of the contemporary female image: to be popular and acceptable in the 1960s, the American woman's image must be split in two.

ASHER, SHELDON, AND IDENTICAL WITCHES, GENIES, AND MAIDS

After directing *The Patty Duke Show* in 1964, William Asher went on to direct *Bewitched*, and in 1965, Sydney Sheldon created the series *I Dream of Jeannie*. Both men clearly transferred their affinities for the twinning trope to each series, as some of the decade's most popular evil twins were, both then and now, the "evil women" of these shows. *Bewitched* was the most popular half-hour series on ABC until 1977, earning 22 Emmy nominations and a spot as one of *TV Guide's* 50 greatest television shows of all time.[50] Neilson ratings placed *I Dream of Jeannie* in the top thirty for multiple seasons.[51] In *Bewitched*, Serena, also played by Elizabeth Montgomery with a dark wig and beauty mark,[52] is the antithesis of Samantha, as she is mischievous, conniving, and wild.

In *I Dream of Jeannie*, Jeannie's sister, also played by Barbara Eden in a dark wig, is the antithesis of Jeannie, as she is flirtatious, progressive, and mean. Thus, in both popular shows, the evil twin is identified through the use of a dark wig—something that aligns these characters immediately with evil, according to the established dark/evil versus light/good trope. The logic behind this trope typically involves a human fear of darkness, in general; thus, darkness is commonly used to depict evil. Even beyond this, though, in an "us vs. them" culture, if the mainstream "us" characters of Samantha and Jeannie are portrayed as good, light-haired women, the obvious option for depicting the evil alter egos as "them" characters, is to use dark hair. To further the message, this trope is implemented explicitly with other female characters, as well. *Bewitched* includes multiple episodes with Darren's ex-girlfriend, Sheila Summers (played by Nancy Kovack), who is a brunette bombshell, constantly trying to steal Darrin away from Samantha. When Kovack is playing this flirtatious, conniving character, which she does in three separate episodes, her hair is dark. But in other episodes, when she plays the also flirtatious female client, Clio Vanita, who literally becomes the monkey of the episode (when Serena transforms her into one), she is blonde. Furthermore, in the episode "Snob in the Grass,"[53] Sheila's dark wig actually falls off, once Samantha uses her magic to strip Sheila of her evil and manipulative ways. The removal of the dark wig parallels the removal of Sheila's

Figure 0.2. Montgomery as Serena in *Bewitched*, PictureLux / The Hollywood Archive / Alamy Stock Photo

evil abilities, representing the dark/evil and light/good tropes precisely. *I Dream of Jeannie* applies the same treatment to the threatening female characters of the series, in addition to sister Jeannie. In "The Americanization of Jeannie,"[54] for example, Jeannie and Tony are at dinner together. The restaurant's entertainment involves a sexy Arabian dancer with black hair. Soon, the dancer begins flirting with Tony, forcing Jeannie to intervene.

Other popular series of the decade used these tropes in similar ways. In *Gilligan's Island*, Eva Grubb is a dark-haired "twin" of movie star Ginger Grant (both roles played by Tina Louise), who has left civilization for a deserted island because men

Figure 0.3. Tina Louise as Ginger (left) and Dawn Wells as Mary Ann (right) in *Gilligan's Island*, PictureLux / The Hollywood Archive / Alamy Stock Photo

are not attracted to her. The island group members give her a makeover, and with new hair, dress, and makeup, she resembles Ginger precisely. Once Eva gets a taste of being beautiful, though, she begins to scheme about assuming Ginger's identity and running away.

In *The Brady Bunch*, housekeeper Alice Nelson decides to take a vacation and asks her twin cousin, Emma (both roles played by Ann B. Davis), to fill in for her while she is gone. Emma has darker hair, wears darker clothes, has a deeper voice, and wears deep red lipstick. As a former Master Sergeant, Emma is domineering, harsh, and inflexible—the complete opposite of Alice. In the end, the Bradys are very glad to see Emma leave and are thrilled when Alice returns.

Figure 0.4.   Ann B. Davis as Alice in *The Brady Bunch*, PictureLux / The Hollywood Archive / Alamy Stock Photo

Finally, even though I use the original *Doctor Who* series to demonstrate how the female evil twins of British television differ from American depictions, the example still uses the dark/light trope. In the episode "Inferno," the professor's assistant scientist, Liz Shaw, has an identical counterpart (both roles played by Caroline John) in a parallel space-time continuum, a "twin world." In this twin world, evil Liz has short dark hair, and she wears tall black boots, a military uniform, leather gloves, and a gun. However, even though her physical traits tend to model the ones used by American examples, she *and* her good counterpart are *both* educated and occupy highly respected positions in the public, versus private, sphere—a portrayal that utilizes the dark/light trope, while differing greatly from American examples.

THE TELEVISION WRITERS OF THE 1960S

Many of the episodes in these series share the same handful of writers. Sheldon and Asher were clearly very influential with regard to all of the evil twins of the 1960s, having both worked so closely on *The Patty Duke Show* (as writer and director, respectively), which appears to have inspired many of the subsequent representations. Asher moved on to direct *Bewitched*, and Sheldon later created and wrote for *I Dream of Jeannie*. In addition to his actual name, Sheldon also wrote under the pseudonyms Christopher Golato and Allan Devon, which means he wrote even more episodes of these series than one might initially suspect. Thus, his influence is significant on the three heavyweights of this study—*The Patty Duke Show, Bewitched*, and *I Dream of Jeannie*, to say the least. But many television writers worked on more than one of the series analyzed herein. Joanna Lee, who wrote the "All About Eva"[55] episode of *Gilligan's Island*, also wrote episodes of *I Dream of Jeannie* and *The Brady Bunch*. Ed Jurist was a frequent writer of episodes for both *Bewitched* and *The Patty Duke Show*. Married couple Peggy Chantler Dick and Douglas Dick wrote for *Bewitched* and *I Dream of Jeannie*, and couple Leo and Pauline Townsend wrote for *Bewitched* and *The Patty Duke Show*. Michael Morris was a prominent writer on *The Brady Bunch* and *Bewitched*. Bernie Kahn wrote episodes for *Bewitched* (with Lila Garrett) and for *The Brady Bunch*; Joel Rapp also wrote an episode with Lila Garret for *Bewitched*, in addition to his work on *The Patty Duke Show* and *Gilligan's Island*. Arnold Horwitt wrote for both *The Patty Duke Show* and *I Dream of Jeannie*, and Arthur Julian and John L. Greene both individually wrote for *Bewitched* and *I Dream of Jeannie*. Sherwood Schwartz, the creator and producer of *Gilligan's Island* (1964) and *The Brady Bunch* (1969), collaborated with Sol Saks, the creator of *Bewitched*, on multiple projects. Last, the very first "Sister Jeannie" episode of *I Dream of Jeannie* was not written by Sheldon, but by James S. Henerson, who wrote almost half of the evil-twin *Jeannie* episodes and several *Bewitched* episodes. Henerson also wrote a film titled *The Feminist and the Fuzz*,[56] starring Barbara Eden. The movie was about a male chauvinist police officer (David Hartman) and a feminist doctor (Barbara Eden) finding that the only way they can both afford the "perfect apartment," which they have arrived to tour, coincidentally at the same time, is by becoming roommates. The film is telling regarding Henerson's connection to sixties feminism. Henerson wrote the first evil-twin *I Dream of Jeannie* episode in 1967 and *The Feminist and the Fuzz* in 1971. The film confirms Henerson's awareness of the 1960s feminist dialogue, which would certainly have included Friedan's theories—something discussed in detail in chapter 3. It is worth noting here that *Bewitched* employed far more female writers than any other series—a detail that may have had something to do with Montgomery's influence—and in the fifth chapter, the differences between the female writers/co-writers involved in all of the series (Joanna Lee, Barbara Avedon, Shirley Gordon, Lila Garrett, Pauline Townsend, and Peggy Chantler Dick) and the male writers are analyzed as revealing pieces of evidence concerning the influence of Friedan's text.

FEMINISM AND TELEVISION

The Patty Duke Show (1963–1966), *Bewitched* (1964–1972), *Gilligan's Island* (1964–1967), *I Dream of Jeannie* (1965–1970), and *The Brady Bunch* (1969–1974)[57] all use the twinning trope to deal with issues of feminism and identity in similar ways, indicating that Friedan's "split" theory was surely a part of the 1960s popular culture dialogue in America. Using this trope, the shows claim that women who are not perpetually self-sacrificing must belong to the counterculture, and in a decade defined by binary oppositions, if housewifery is depicted as "good," these characters must be "evil." Regarding Friedan's split, whereas scholars like Leibman and Douglas have suggested that some of these shows (e.g., *Bewitched* and *I Dream of Jeannie*) paralleled the changing social climate in America with characters that embodied women's emerging social and sexual powers, I argue these shows furthered the feminine mystique through depictions of both the split of the American woman image, and of the "voice" stirring within housewives/women of the era, claiming to want more than husbands, children, and home.

METHODOLOGY

As a faculty member in English, I have been trained to read "texts," so I regard these television episodes as "texts." Thus, textual analysis underpins my methodology—an approach maintaining the idea that these texts produce meaning, rather than merely reflect meaning—searching for patterns and inconsistencies in the blocking, dialogue, character, plot, mise-en-scène, and iconography of each series. I am not calling my methodology "close textual analysis" because I do not analyze features such as shot frame and distance to find meaning (even though I do note that *The Brady Bunch* episode uses a canted shot during the montage of Emma's controlling activities during her stay, indicating the dysfunction of the scenario). My approach is grounded in the belief that, as Leibman notes, "film and television are similarly involved in a form of sophisticated mythmaking, relying on transhistorical modes of storytelling which traditionally focus on areas of social concern."[58] In order to understand the way representation works, the act of creating visuals, including anything from television to advertisements, must be understood as "signifying practice." As Stuart Hall puts it in his work, *Representation: Cultural Representations and Signifying Practices,* "meaning does not inhere *in* things, in the world. It is constructed, produced. It is the result of signifying practice—a practice that *produces* meaning, that *makes things mean.*"[59] Hall uses Swiss linguist Saussure's theory to explain that meaning is never completely fixed, and individuals of a common culture must actively interpret.[60] Thus, the series I analyze herein have been chosen not just because of their enormous popularity in the sixties and their longevity in syndication, all of which indicates the collective influence the shows had on American popular culture, but because they appear to be in conversation with Friedan about issues of social concern, gender performance, and mythmaking. In conducting my research, I was struck by something Paul A. Cantor said in his book, *Gilligan Unplugged: Pop Culture in the Age of Globalization,* regarding the work we all do in the field of Cultural Studies. He finds that one of the faults of Cultural Studies is its "tendency to impose a kind of homogeneity on the phenomena it discusses, viewing all TV programs, for example, as telling the same sad tale of racist and sexist stereotyping."[61] I sincerely hope the same for my study, as I have tried to allow the texts to maintain the same sort of artistic integrity Cantor describes, without forcing my own prescription on the episodes. This is the reason I begin with Sheldon in this introduction, as his influence on these texts seems to align much more with that of an *auteur* than the typical community approach to television. To borrow Cantor's words once more, "Although I am interested in the effect of particular TV programs on society, I am much more concerned with them as artistic forms that embody and express distinctive views of the world."[62] I am concerned with these programs as artistic forms expressing views of the world, but I am also interested in the function they perform to program consumer-viewers. I have organized the chapters by series, covering each show in a separate chapter. Within each chapter, I analyze how these evil-twin characters display the desire for a sense of separate self, a need for self-service and independence, and a longing to maintain and enjoy personal interests, while good twins are in constant service of others.

Ultimately, I argue that the evil alter egos of 1960s television serve as manifestations of Friedan's split theory.[63] Each series includes episodes featuring female characters encountering identical dark-haired counterparts played by the same actresses. I contend that these characters are portrayed as "evil women" because they are embodiments of Friedan's text and are thus visual constructions of the evil manifestations of that voice when unsuppressed. Using the traits identified by Friedan and other scholars as being indicative of the suppressed voice, of the "devil inside," I analyze the ways in which these alter-ego characters embody the desire for separate self and independence through loose inhibitions, career interests, political interests, intellectual prowess, and assertiveness. Regarding loose inhibitions, I investigate how the evil alter egos entertain and explore their own personal interests and how they are portrayed as being excessively selfish and lacking self-control, rather than merely desiring a sense of separate self—desiring an opportunity to pursue their own interests. Also within this category, I analyze moments when the alter egos, as single women, are often attempting to seduce men and, at times, steal them away from other women, an activity that conveys the message that single women are unhappy and dissatisfied, while married women are content and fulfilled. For career interests, I examine how the dialogue of the good twin in each example frequently reflects her happiness, contentment, and satisfaction in roles of service, while the evil twin pursues various forms of career advancement, from Naval officers to stage performers, by which the evil twins attempt to dominate the public sphere just as their opposites are content to serve in the private sphere. Political interests include everything from evil twins serving as elected officials to performing grassroots campaign efforts to shape public policy and opinion. In the category "Intellectual Prowess," I include travel and culture, in addition to more formal types of education and examples of knowledge-seeking. In other words, using this category, I am claiming that the alter egos, in being depicted as both intelligent and manipulative, are confirming Friedan's assessment that American popular culture regards intelligence and education in women as indicators of the evil of independence, as traits belonging to the evil side of the split. The final category of assertiveness is embodied by the evil twins throughout all series. When the evil counterparts want something, they immediately, and often impulsively, pursue it, and all characters resist being told what to do in almost any capacity. The evil twins often caution males against trying to dominate them; that said, the episodes portray their intentions as being more manipulative and controlling, rather than strong and self-aware.

Chapter 1 analyzes the thirty-six episodes of the first season of *The Patty Duke Show*, identifying the ways in which Patty's character reflects loose inhibitions (e.g., displaying a lack of self-control, a desire to chase boys, a feisty temper, and a need to be independent), career interests (e.g., getting a job at the Shake Shop, starting her own fashion company, charging for predictions as a fortune teller, and organizing a babysitting service), political interests (e.g., being elected to leadership positions), and assertiveness (e.g., insisting she be chosen for certain roles and tasks). Chapter 2 focuses on the twenty-two *Bewitched* episodes featuring Serena, analyzing how her character reflects loose inhibitions (e.g., seducing men, dressing sexy, showing a lack of self-control, desiring independence, and being against motherhood), career interests (e.g., getting a job at an ice cream parlor, being in the Navy, entering various competitions, and performing regularly), political interests (e.g., organizing and participating in a riot and "love-in"), intellectual prowess (e.g., having a master's degree, and being exceptionally knowledgeable about art, wine, and travel), and assertiveness (e.g., instructing Darrin never to tell her what to do or to "paw" at her). Chapter 3 addresses the nine *I Dream of Jeannie* episodes that feature her twin sister Jeannie, who also displays traits of loose inhibition, career interests, political interests, intellectual prowess, and assertiveness. Chapter 4 analyzes *The Brady Bunch* episode "Sergeant Emma" and the *Gilligan's Island* episode "All About Eva" using the same five categories, and then examines the *Dr. Who* episode "Inferno" as a comparison between American and non-American examples. At the end of each of these series-analysis chapters, I include sections of conclusions. Since the thrust of my argument involves the extent to which these episodes reflected connections to Friedan and to consumerism, my conclusions will focus mostly on the different functions of the twins in each series—the evil twin is always working within the public sphere, whether that means travel, career, or politics, while the good twin finds all that she needs in the private sphere. This is an important distinction because the more an episode can tether a housewife/housekeeper to the needs of her household, the more aware she becomes of the necessity to buy appropriate products to meet those needs; this practice programs her as a better consumer. Following these analyses, in Chapter 5, I explore the differences between female-written and male-written depictions of the twin characters and their relationships with each other. The distinction of male versus female writing is especially important considering Friedan's words on this matter with regard to the American woman image in magazines. In trying to understand the shift in the American popular culture career woman image, first as spirited, then as evil, she came to an important realization:

> I found a clue one morning, sitting in the office of a women's magazine editor—a woman who, older than I, remembers the days when the old image was being created, and who had watched it being displaced. The old image of the spirited career girl was largely created by writers and editors who were women, she told me. The new image of woman as housewife-mother has been largely created by writers and editors who are men.[64]

After WWII, as women were urged to leave the workforce and return to the home, women's magazine editors became largely male—men whose jobs were to identify and provide what female readers, mostly housewives, would most like to encounter in these magazines. Friedan remembers a meeting with some of these male editors, as they described their assumptions regarding the needs of their female readers. One unnamed male editor said the following: "Our readers are housewives, full time. They're not interested in the broad public issues of the day. They are not interested in national or international affairs. They are only interested in the family and the home."[65] This is an important point because it highlights the differences between male and female engagement with Friedan's text and with visual cultures in general.

All of these series include episodes written by both males and females, sometimes as duos and sometimes independently. Of the 139 *I Dream of Jeannie* episodes, five were written or co-written by women, representing roughly 3.5 percent of the entire series. Of the 104 *Patty Duke Show* episodes, only two were co-written by females, representing 1.9 percent of the series. The low percentages of female-written *I Dream of Jeannie* and *Patty Duke Show* episodes shouldn't automatically indicate that Sheldon, creator of and writer for both series, was against hiring women. Sheldon actually wrote so many of the episodes himself that it greatly diminished the need, in general, to hire any other writers—a fact that further supports his strong, single-handed influence on the twinning trope of 1960s television, in general. (In fact, it is worth noting that this situation also existed for Amy Sherman-Palladino, creator of and writer for *The Marvelous Mrs. Maisel*,[66] a twenty-first century show that is discussed in the fifth chapter. In negotiations with the network over her first hit, *Gilmore Girls*, one of her requests involved hiring more writers, so that she wasn't burdened with the task of writing every episode—much like Sheldon. Her request was ultimately denied by the network and her time with *Gilmore Girls* ended there, but she soon created *The Marvelous Mrs. Maisel*—a current award-winning period piece that serves to address some of these issues.) Of the 117 episodes of *The Brady Bunch*, twelve were written or co-written by female writers, representing 10.3 percent of the series. Unfortunately, none of the evil-twin episodes of any of these three series was written or co-written by women, which makes a comparison of male and female perspectives nearly impossible with *I Dream of Jeannie*, *The Patty Duke Show*, or *The Brady Bunch*. *Bewitched* and *Gilligan's Island*, however, provide different case studies. Of the 254 *Bewitched* episodes, thirty-four are written or co-written by women, representing about 13.38 percent of the series—the highest percentage of all shows analyzed in this study—and of the twenty-two evil-twin episodes, five are written or co-written by women, representing roughly 14.2 percent of those episodes. Of the 98 *Gilligan's Island* episodes, seven are written or co-written by female writers, representing only 7.14 percent of the series, but the one female evil-twin episode, "All About Eva," was written by a woman, Joanna Lee. This makes a comparison of gender perspectives possible, and considering many of these shows ran concurrently for many years, it is also possible to compare female-written evil-twin episodes of *Bewitched* and *Gilligan's Island* to male-written evil-twin episodes of the other series.

When evil-twin episodes are written or co-written by women, the twins are presented less as an oppositional binary and more as a compatible, often symbiotic binary, where they are still depicted as opposites, but opposites who work together and, in some cases, need each other. Therefore, the female perspective reveals an image of the American woman that is both good and evil, self-serving and self-sacrificing, career-minded and homemaker. These female writers seem to indicate that the image of the American woman created by popular culture should be less of a strict oppositional binary, as male writers seemed to prefer, where women must fall into one side or the other of Friedan's split, and more of a complex combination of these qualities. And just as these female-written episodes depict evil twins who often rely on and need each other, they are implying the same balance exists within the American woman. Male writers seem to create twins with qualities that are so oppositional, they usually can't function effectively in each other's worlds. I argue that this has much to do with the male interpretation of Friedan's split, with the evil side—the career-minded, politically interested, assertive, self-serving woman—desiring power and control, rather than equality. Incidentally, this reflects a commonly held misnomer of feminism in general, that feminists want to control and have power over men instead of seeking equality. Male-written depictions of evil twins reflect and produce the idea that women who fall on the evil side of the split are ultimately controlling and power-hungry and rejecting of domesticity and that they, consequently, serve as warnings. The evil twins almost always end up alone—something that even occurs with the twenty-first century example that I include in the fifth chapter, *The Marvelous Mrs. Maisel* (something that speaks to the persistence of representation). Thus, the warning conveyed to women through these depictions involves the idea that self-service and a rejection of domesticity will increase the potential of spinsterhood, while self-sacrifice guarantees companionship and security. Even though the female writers of 1960s television made strides regarding popular culture's image of the American women, by depicting Jeannie, Samantha, and Cathy as utterly fulfilled in their service, and their twins as perpetually restless and dissatisfied, the evil twins, like Midge Maisel, are left to serve as warnings: indulge that evil voice, and one might end up unhappy and alone.

NOTES

1. Katharine Bullock, "Orientalism on Television: A Case Study of I Dream of Jeannie," *ReOrient* Vol. 4, No. 1 (Autumn 2018), 4. Bullock cites the 2003 work *The Audience in Everyday Life: Living in a Media World* by S.E. Bird as her source for this information.

2. *Bewitched*, season 6, episode 19, "Tabitha's Very Own Samantha," written by Shirley Gordon and directed by William Asher, January 1970.

3. Walter Metz, *Bewitched* (Detroit: Wayne State UP, 2007). In *Bewitched* the book, Walter Metz discusses on page four how the *Bewitched* magical characters and special effects would have appealed to children, which is partly why it was so popular with younger audiences.

4. Susan J. Douglas, *Where the Girls Are: Growing Up Female with the Mass Media* (New York: Three Rivers Press, 1995), 138.

5. Betty Friedan, *The Feminine Mystique,* Tenth Anniversary Edition (New York: W.W. Norton & Company, Inc., 1974), 44. Friedan claimed that after 1949, society determined that fulfillment for women could be achieved only through the role of the housewife-mother. Furthermore, she mentioned the woman's loss of self-identity in society's rush for the security of togetherness.

6. Nina C. Leibman, *Living Room Lectures: The Fifties Family in Film and Television* (Austin, TX: University of Texas Press, 1995), 86.

7. Kristi Humphreys, "Supernatural Housework," in *Home Sweat Home*, edited by Mimi Choi and Elizabeth Patton (Lanham, MD: Scarecrow Press, 2014), 107.

8. Leibman discusses this creation of the housewife in *Living Room Lectures*, 86.

9. Mary Ann Doane, *Femmes Fatales: Feminism, Film Theory, Psychoanalysis* (New York: Routledge, 1991), 2–3.

10. *Double Indemnity,* directed by Billy Wilder, 1944.

11. *Sunset Boulevard,* directed by Billy Wilder, 1950.

12. *Vertigo,* directed by Alfred Hitchcock, 1958.

13. Friedan, *The Feminine Mystique*, 32.

14. Ibid., 27

15. Ibid., 33

16. Ibid., 46

17. Ibid., 46

18. Ibid., 61

19. Kristi Humphreys, *Housework and Gender in American Television: Coming Clean* (Lanham, MD: Lexington Books, 2015). I argue that when representations of housework are viewed as maternal practice—the act of preservation—strength is inherent in the activity of service. I do not mean to disagree with this stance here.

20. Friedan, *Feminine Mystique*, 58

21. Leibman, *Living Room Lectures*,174.

22. Ibid., 174.

23. Friedan, "Television and the Feminine Mystique," in *American Decades Primary Sources*, edited by Cynthia Rose, vol. 7: 1960–1969, Gale, 2004, 396–399.

24. Metz, *Bewitched*,18.

25. *I Dream of Jeannie*, season 1, episode 8, "The Americanization of Jeannie," written by Arnold Horwitt, directed by Gene Nelson, November 1965.

26. Metz, *Bewitched*, 42

27. Ibid., 77. Metz makes this argument about *Bewitched* specifically, but I argue that it can be said of all of the shows included in this study.

28. Lynn Spigel and Michael Curtin, eds. *The Revolution Wasn't Televised: Sixties Television and Social Conflict* (New York: Routledge, 1997), 2.

29. *The Dark Mirror*, written by Nunnally Johnson (screenplay) and Vladimir Pozner (story), directed by Robert Siodmak, starring Olivia de Havilland, 1946.

30. *A Stolen Life*, written by Catherine Turney (screenplay), Margaret Burnell Wilder (adaptation), Karel J. Benes (book), directed by Curtis Bernhardt, starring Bette Davis, 1946.

31. *Dead Ringer*, written by Albert Beich (screenplay), Oscar Millard (screenplay), and Rian James (story), directed by Paul Henreid, starring Bette Davis, 1964.

32. *Twins of Evil*, written by Tudor Gates, directed by John Hough, starring Peter Cushing, 1971.

33. David Marc, *Comic Visions: Television Comedy and American Culture* (Boston: Unwin Hyman, 1989), 139.

34. *Bonanza*, season 4, episode 27, "Mirror of a Man," written by A.I. Bezzerides, directed by Lewis Allen, March 1963.

35. *Star Trek*, season 2, episode 4, "Mirror, Mirror," written by Jerome Bixby, directed by Marc Daniels, October 1967.

36. It is worth noting that both examples of "Mirror of a Man" and "Mirror, Mirror" utilize titles that reflect the psychiatrist's dialogue in the aforementioned film *The Dark Mirror*, when he concludes that twins are reflections of each other: "everything in reverse."

37. *Get Smart*, season 5, episode 21, "And Only Two Ninety-Nine," written by Arne Sultan, directed by Don Adams, February 1970.

38. Marc, *Comic Visions*, 139.

39. William L. O'Neill, *Coming Apart: An Informal History of the 1960s* (New York: Times Books, 1971), 196.

40. Paul Attallah "The Unworthy Discourse: Situation Comedy in Television," in *Critiquing the Sitcom*, edited by Joanne Morreale (Syracuse, NY: Syracuse UP, 2003), 91–115, 107.

41. Moya Luckett, "Girl Watchers: Patty Duke and Teen TV," in *The Revolution Wasn't Televised: Sixties Television and Social Conflict*, eds. Lynn Spigel and Michael Curtin (New York: Routledge, 1997), 101.

42. Sydney Sheldon, *The Other Side of Me* (New York: Warner Books, 2005), 210.

43. Friedan, *The Feminine Mystique,* 210–211.

44. *The Patty Duke Show*, season 1, episode 5, "The Birds and the Bees Bit," written by Sidney Sheldon, directed by Stanley Prager, October 1963. Incidentally, Sheldon (as Allan Devon) also wrote an episode of *I Dream of Jeannie* with the same title in 1967.

45. *The Patty Duke Show*, season 1, episode 23, "Are Mothers People," written by Sidney Sheldon, directed by Stanley Prager, February 1964.

46. Leibman discusses these issues in *Living Room Lectures,* saying that this type of housewife "was a career woman after all; it's just that her career was the home and family," 193.

47. Interview can be found on *Youtube* at https://www.youtube.com/watch?v=xsVzEapclRU.

48. Interview can be found in the Television Academy's archives at https://interviews.tele visionacademy.com/interviews/patty-duke.

49. Interview can be found in the Television Academy's archives at https://interviews.tele visionacademy.com/interviews/patty-duke#interview-clips.

50. Denise Lowe, *Women and American Television: An Encyclopedia* (Santa Barbara: ABC-Clio, 1999), 36; Internet Movie Database (http://www.imdb.com/list/ls000996988/).

51. This information was found on *ClassicTVHits.com* at http://classictvhits.com/tvratings/index.htm.

52. In a few of the earlier Serena episodes of *Bewitched*, Serena wears a long, straight blonde wig. This is soon replaced by a short black wig—a change the show maintained through the end of its run.

53. *Bewitched*, season 4, episode 19, "Snob in the Grass," written by Ed Jurist, directed by R. Robert Rosenbaum, January 1968.

54. *I Dream of Jeannie*, season 1, episode 8, "The Americanization of Jeannie," written by Arnold Horwitt, directed by Gene Nelson, November 1965.

55. *Gilligan's Island*, season 3, episode 14, "All About Eva," written by Joanna Lee, directed by Jerry Hopper, December 1966.

56. *The Feminist and the Fuzz*, written by James Henerson, directed by Jerry Paris, starring Barbara Eden, January 1971.

57. The *Doctor Who* series (1963–1989) also uses the twinning trope, but the series is used to discuss the differences between American and non-American depictions of "evil alter egos."

58. Leibman, *Living Room Lectures*, 10.

59. Stuart Hall, ed., *Representation: Cultural Representations and Signifying Practices* (London: Sage, 1997), 24.

60. Ibid., 32.

61. Paul A. Cantor, *Gilligan Unplugged: Pop Culture in the Age of Globalization* (Lanham, MD: Rowman and Littlefield, 2002), xxxiv.

62. Ibid., xli.

63. Friedan, *The Feminine Mystique,* 32.

64. Ibid., 54

65. Ibid., 37.

66. *The Marvelous Mrs. Maisel*, created by Amy Sherman-Palladino, starring Rachel Brosnahan, 2017.

1

The Patty Duke Show

The Patty Duke Show began airing in September of 1963 and ran for three years; it is still enjoying a wide audience in syndication. In the show, Patty Duke plays identical cousins, Patty and Cathy Lane, in addition to identical cousin Betsy Lane in one episode.[1] Sydney Sheldon wrote almost every episode of the entire series, and William Asher produced and directed many of them. The show also starred William Schallert as Martin Lane and Kenneth Lane (Patty's and Cathy's twin fathers, respectively), Jean Byron as Natalie Lane (Patty's mother), Paul O'Keefe as Ross Lane (Patty's brother), and Eddie Applegate as Richard Harrison (Patty's boyfriend). The production team filmed in New York city because the location had more flexible child labor laws, allowing Duke, who was sixteen when the show began, to work more hours. (This is also the reason the unaired pilot depicted the Lane family as living in San Francisco, but the first episode to air had the family living in Brooklyn Heights, New York.) Once Duke turned eighteen, the show was moved to Los Angeles for the final season. This show differs from the others analyzed in the study because Patty and Cathy are teenagers, rather than "adult" women. That means that the behaviors exhibited by Patty, which in all other examples appear on the evil side of the split, could be considered typical behaviors for an American teenager. Still, I include the series here for one main reason: by his own admission, the show's creator, Sheldon, felt that he could only capture the personality of Anne Marie "Patty" Duke—the actual person—by using two characters (or three in one episode) in television, thus furthering, whether intentionally or not, Friedan's claims regarding persistent popular culture images of the American woman. I begin with *The Patty Duke Show* because it is chronologically the first highly popular television example of twinning being used to produce split images of women, and its popularity seems to have galvanized the prevalence of twinning in subsequent television shows. Its influence in this regard is sprawling and significant.

In the show's unaired pilot, as implausible as it may seem, the family is depicted as being completely surprised by the likenesses of the cousins. It seems implausible because Martin and his brother Kenneth are twins, and even though Kenneth works overseas as a foreign correspondent, they appear to be emotionally very close, so it is curious that they don't have some idea of the physical similarities of their teenage nieces. When Cathy arrives, Patty and family are shocked by the fact that they are identical, but the stark differences between the personalities of Patty and Cathy are revealed immediately, with Cathy embodying the good side of the split and Patty embodying the evil side. Patty says, "Separately, we are two girls who have few talents, just like anyone else . . . but together, we are really on the beam. We can be at two different places at the same time." Cathy responds, "But Patty, that isn't honest," and Patty replies, "It is if we don't get caught." Cathy ends the conversation with, "The logic of that escapes me." The pilot portrays Patty as being willing to be dishonest to get what she wants. It also implies that without each other, they are not whole people. As individuals, Patty recognizes they have few talents, but together, they can be much more powerful, even if that means doing the wrong thing. While Cathy wants to display some level of self-control, especially at the cost of being dishonest or irresponsible, Patty sees only the importance of not getting caught—a trait that leads one to interpret many of Patty's actions as being of loose inhibition.

Before delving into the categories, though, mainly because of Sheldon's words on Marilyn Monroe and the split identities of women, it is essential to discuss the one episode in which Patty Duke plays three identical cousins, Patty, Cathy, and Betsy—a character that was clearly inspired by Marilyn Monroe's persona. Monroe is quite possibly one of the most popular examples of the split image that was identified by Friedan in 1963.[2] During a time when it was deemed improper for women to be sexual, Monroe was the quintessential bombshell sex symbol. Yet, this persona was balanced by a shyness and modesty that did not seem to match the persona—something that surely served to make her sexuality more acceptable in the fifties. Thus, just as Sheldon's perception of Monroe on their date in 1956 was that it was as though he "were having dinner with two different people" because "what she was saying seemed so incongruous coming from this beautiful young woman,"[3] her modesty, shyness, soft-spoken nature, and innocence seemed incongruous to the public with her astonishing sexuality. Furthermore, one can find any number of interviews where reporters ask Monroe about the various "Marilyns" they encounter. For example, when she met the press in the early sixties, after taking a year off from Hollywood to study acting in New York, she was asked by a reporter if the public can expect this to be a "new Marilyn."[4] She was quick to answer that she is always the same person and that only her suit has changed. Her desire to be a serious actress and career woman seemed incongruous with her role as a sex symbol. And in her final interview, just days before her death, Richard Meryman, Associate Editor for *Life* magazine, reported on his experience with her that day.[5] He claimed to have witnessed a "roller coaster of moods" during their conversation, finding that she would laugh at odd and unexpected moments. Ultimately, her personality was incongruous with her persona. These examples are consistent with Sheldon's perception of Monroe as "two different people." In this way, Monroe embodies Friedan's observations precisely—the image of woman in popular culture is split in two.

I begin this chapter with a discussion of Monroe because of the episode "The Perfect Hostess," which seems to present Sheldon's overall perception of a "split Marilyn"[6] and split female identities, in general. In this episode, Duke plays a third identical cousin, Betsy, who is the daughter of Martin's cousin Gaylord in Atlanta. Betsy's characterization is clearly modeled after Marilyn Monroe, as she has blonde hair, is considered very sexy, claims to be shy, speaks in a whispery tone, attracts the attention of all the boys in town, dates many, and pretends to be different people to different individuals.

In the episode, when Patty and Cathy start helping Betsy unpack from her trip, Patty finds a picture of a good-looking boy. Patty asks if he is her "steady." Betsy replies, "No, that's just a boy I date." Patty begins pulling out additional pictures of boys, and Betsy claims to be dating all of them. When Betsy appears to miss the boys for a moment, Patty says, "Betsy, tomorrow we'll take you to the Shake Shop to meet a bunch of the local boys." The next day, they go to the Shake Shop, and Betsy is flirting with Cathy's boyfriend, George, who asks Betsy to go to a movie with him. The next day, Patty and Cathy go back to the Shake Shop, and they see Betsy at a

Figure 1.1. Patty Duke as cousin Betsy in "The Perfect Hostess,"
The Patty Duke Show, **Disney ABC Television Group / Getty Images**

table with Patty's boyfriend, Richard. When the girls confront Betsy at home, she apologizes, and Patty says, "Don't worry about it; you can't help being irresistible." Betsy begins to pretend to be different people to Cathy and Patty, encouraging both of them to turn on the other. Betsy uses their differences in personality and interests to divide them, while they normally, as Patty says, "get along great!" Once Patty and Cathy realize what is happening, Patty decides to pretend to be Cathy when she talks to Betsy, to ascertain what she is saying to each of them behind their backs. Betsy's nefarious intentions are thus revealed, and she is angry and embarrassed.

The true significance of this episode, though, is the message it furthers about good girls being family girls and evil ones being family-less, whether that means not having a husband, children, or even parents. This is a trend that will remain consistent for all of the evil twins analyzed in this book. After talking with Betsy about her actions, Martin tries to explain things to an angry Patty, saying, "Patty, you and Cathy have every reason to be furious with Betsy, but I wish you would try to understand her a little . . . she is just a very lonely girl. Maybe she has plenty of dates, but what she doesn't seem to have is a family." Martin explains that Betsy had hoped to make Cathy so uncomfortable living there that she would leave, and perhaps Betsy could stay and finally have a family. In this way, the episode references Monroe on several levels and clearly represents and reproduces Friedan's split theory and Sheldon's perception of women as "two different people."[7] Like the character Betsy, Monroe had a difficult childhood, living in and out of foster homes and orphanages during most of her adolescence. She married at the age of 16, in order to avoid being sent back to the orphanage. She worked as a housewife to a military husband for a few years but ultimately divorced when her husband did not want her to model or work—something she earnestly desired. Monroe began family-less as an orphan, but when she married, thus beginning a family and embracing the acceptable roles for a mid-century woman of the era—the roles of housewife and potential mother—Monroe rejected them; she swapped this existence for one embracing the unacceptable roles for a mid-century woman—the roles of career woman and sex symbol. She navigates both binaries of Friedan's split in a matter of years, and when Monroe is family-less, she takes on the attributes of the evil side of the split. Incidentally, it is important to note that Monroe often spoke in interviews about how much she wanted to be a part of the roles on the good side of this split, which might have contributed to how she maintained so much popularity with her identity as an unmarried female sex symbol in the 1950s.[8] Like Monroe, Betsy's ultimate flaw, which leads her to be a sexual individual, date many boys, and succumb to insecurities, is a lack of family. This lack of familial connections are the flaws embodied in each of the evil alter egos analyzed in the study. When Betsy is removed from the trio, which is the case for all other episodes, it is clear that Patty represents and reproduces the qualities of the evil side of the split. Whereas Cathy wants to stay home and read, clean, or wash her hair (qualities that are among those mid-century housewives—those on the good side of the split—were expected to enjoy and embrace), Patty wants to go to parties, kiss boys, wear trendy clothes, start her own businesses, and in general, be a person of loose inhibition (activities that are among those the self-serving women—those on the evil side of the split—were perceived to enjoy and embrace).

LOOSE INHIBITIONS

Even the lyrics to the show's opening song describe Patty's loose inhibitions: "Cathy adores a minuet, the Ballets Russes, a Crepe Suzette, but Patty likes to rock and roll, a hot dog makes her lose control."[9] Loose inhibitions are depicted through the character Patty as qualities of dishonesty, sexuality, trendy interests, sneakiness, jealousy, messiness, and in general, any qualities that represent a lack of self-control and a desire to be self-serving. As I've mentioned, in the pilot episode, Cathy arrives to the Lane house from the airport before the rest of the family gets home. Once she is inside the house, the doorbell rings; she answers and unknowingly finds Richard, Patty's boyfriend. Thinking she is Patty, Richard kisses her on the forehead twice and Cathy slaps him both times. The episode immediately establishes the sexual differences of the girls. Richard is accustomed to greeting Patty with kisses, indicating kissing is something Patty does often. Cathy, however, is much more modest in her relationships. Later, the housekeeper thinks she sees Patty (who is actually Cathy) and asks her to clean her room because she can't walk in the room without stepping on the Paul Anka records scattered on the floor. Cathy hasn't heard of Paul Anka, who was already an internationally successful singer/songwriter by the 1960s. Even with his enormous success, though, Cathy has not heard of the entertainer, indicating her ineptitude regarding popular culture. Thus, the split is established from the beginning. Patty allows herself to get into low-brow, popular teenage music and even enjoy finding trouble in the public sphere, while Cathy is completely unaware of the trends and prefers to stay away from trouble by remaining in the private sphere. Of course, the episode ends with Cathy doing the responsible thing and cleaning Patty's room for her, even without having made the mess herself—an act of service that almost any wife or mother, and image thereof, understands. Even in the beginning of the series—and without her character being a wife or mother—Cathy takes on the servile qualities of the good side of the spit, while Patty takes on the self-serving qualities of the evil side. Subsequent episodes further these qualities for Patty through loose inhibitions.

In the episode "The Elopement,"[10] the Lane family is trying to send Martin on a fishing vacation for his anniversary. In the meantime, Martin is writing an editorial that criticizes the parents of teenagers who get married. Patty decides to obtain the fishing license for her dad with her own money, but when Martin's boss, Mr. Castle (John McGiver), sees Patty at the license office with Richard, he assumes they have just filed for a marriage license, not a fishing license. Castle tells Martin, who promptly begins to interrogate Cathy about it because Cathy "has a built-in lie detector: she hiccups when she lies." Consequently, when Martin asks questions about Patty's whereabouts, in an effort to keep the fishing trip a secret, Cathy lies by saying she does not know where Patty is and then hiccups. Patty is thus depicted as sneaky, while Cathy is honest to the extent that her body has a physical reaction to dishonesty. Later in the episode, when Martin learns it is Richard whom Castle believes Patty is marrying, Martin admits, "Patty is rebellious, but Richard is ridiculous." Patty is depicted as independent and driven (buying the fishing license on her own with her own money), yet interpreted as rebellious and sneaky, and Cathy is depicted as honest and controlled (unable to cover for Patty successfully), yet interpreted as dependent and easily manipulated.

The episode "The House Guest"[11] presents the first phone call made from Martin's twin brother, Kenneth (also played by William Schallert). Kenneth calls from Paris to check on Cathy, and Cathy tells him the Lanes are taking very good care of her, even fattening her up just a bit. She hands the phone to Patty, who tells her uncle that she is turning Cathy into "a real swinger." Kenneth is also calling to tell the family that their Aunt Pauline (Ilka Chase) is going to visit them. Aunt Pauline is a wealthy, single, and eccentric woman, whom the family dreads seeing because of her harsh personality and strange tastes in modern art. Patty admits that she hopes she doesn't lose her temper with Aunt Pauline, and Cathy says that she has a sensible solution to that problem. Whenever she and her father feel they are getting upset, they have a code. They say, "It is T time" (indicating "temper time," yet heard by others as "tea time") to get them out of the situation. Throughout the episode, Patty and other family members get frustrated and argue with Aunt Pauline, but Cathy continues to remind them about "tea time." She displays restraint and self-control, while Patty is short-fused and uncontrolled.

In another episode, "Double Date,"[12] Natalie is requiring Patty to get a flu shot, but Patty is resisting because she is throwing a party that evening and does not want to feel sick. Natalie schedules the flu shot, but Patty gets Cathy to go to the doctor for her, to pose as Patty. Cathy had planned to attempt to get out of the shot, but before she could succeed, the doctor sticks her with the needle. Later, Cathy gets quite ill and doesn't feel well enough to attend the dance. She worries that her date will be upset that they, as a couple, can't compete in the dance-off. In an effort to repair the damage she has caused, Patty says she will portray both of them for the evening. However, when she wins the dance-off as Cathy (with Cathy's date), Patty gets angry and reveals the entire charade. Patty is depicted here as being cunning, dishonest, and ultimately, uncaring. But without having to interpret her through a lens of the split, one could interpret her actions differently. For example, when she asked Cathy to go to the doctor for her, she wasn't asking Cathy to get the shot for her. It is likely Patty had been planning this party for quite a while, and it is understandable that she would want to remain healthy in order to be a good hostess—something a mother would also want for her daughter. Her solution to send Cathy to evade the shot altogether, could serve as evidence of her resourcefulness and determination. Similarly, when she decides to portray both cousins during the dance, she is putting aside her own need to enjoy herself, so that she is able to maintain Cathy's relationship with her date for her. Then, when she wins the dance-off as Cathy and gets angry, this could be interpreted as a sign of her drive to succeed. However, the interpretation left with viewers is that Patty's duplicity and jealousy are all signs of a lack of self-control and a desire to be selfish—all qualities that, according to 1960s popular culture, lead to trouble.

Similarly, the "How to be Popular"[13] episode opens with Patty hosting another dance party. Cathy is on the sidelines observing and trying to learn how to do the trendy dance called "the hammer" that everyone is performing. Patty looks concerned over Cathy's inability to do the dance, which appears to be quite simple, so Richard says, "Maybe she is anti-boy." Patty replies, "No red-blooded American girl is anti-boy." Then, a boy approaches Cathy and asks if she wants to do "the hammer" with him. She asks if they could simply do a waltz, and he replies, "Boy, you're older than you look." Patty asks the boy again to go back and pay some attention to Cathy, but he says, "Get someone else to water your wallflowers." This episode is interesting because it is clear that Patty is trying to be thoughtful. She wants Cathy to enjoy the dance and is doing all that she can to help her cousin. Still, her actions are interpreted as serving to cause more trouble. For example, when Richard assumes Cathy is "anti-boy" because she isn't able to do the trendy dance and find a partner, Patty disagrees because "no red-blooded American girl is anti-boy." First, Cathy wasn't raised in America—something of which a concerned Patty would be very aware. This depiction of Patty presents her caring about Cathy's happiness, while simultaneously being oblivious to her situation and needs. Second, Richard assumes that Cathy must be "anti-boy" because she isn't dancing with a partner. Cathy represents the good side of the split, which means that she must be dependent on a male in order to comply with the expectations of the split. When she doesn't, the characters "other" her, interpreting her as strange.[14] Finally, as with most of the other evil alter egos, Cathy falls on the good side of the split because she is unaware of the trends in dance, fashion, and music—knowledge that almost all of the evil twins pride themselves on flaunting. This unawareness is often depicted as Cathy not being adept in "swinging American customs," but through the lens of the split, the interpretation has more to do with Cathy being a good, house-loving, service-loving, family-loving girl who is content to let Patty be everything else.

The first episode in the *Patty Duke* series to be written by someone other than Sheldon was "Slumber Party,"[15] which also introduced the first female co-writer to the show, Pauline Townsend (co-writing with Leo Townsend). The differences observed in this episode are significant and will be an important part of the discussion in the fifth chapter regarding the contrast between male-written episodes and female-written episodes. Similar to Cathy's inexperience with the popular singer Paul Anka, with the popular dance "the hammer," and with popular fashion in other episodes, here, Cathy has never been to a slumber party and has no idea what people do at one. Upon hearing this, Patty responds, "You've lived here too long. It's time to get acquainted with some of our swinging American customs." The party begins with all of the girls, except Cathy, showing each other the popular dances. They have rollers in their hair, so when "the boys" ring the doorbell, they ask Cathy, who has no rollers and is doing no dancing, to go answer the door for them while they remove their curlers and attempt to look presentable. When Cathy talks with the boys, she tells them the girls had to "get some things out of their hair." The boys are told to leave, and the girls return to the living room. One friend asks, "Can you picture our history teacher having a slumber party?" Patty responds, "Oh, 'Tuttle the Terrible?' I can't picture her doing anything. She was born an old maid. You would think she could make Roman history a little more interesting. I mean, she was there." As with other episodes, here, Patty is depicted as having a command of America's "swinging customs": she flaunts the popular dances, follows the trends in hair, has no problem creating nicknames for her teachers, and ultimately is depicted as thinking Cathy would be happier if she would learn to be more like her—another shared trait of almost all of the female evil alter egos of the decade.

Finally, in returning to the episode "The Perfect Hostess," when Cathy arrives home with groceries, she finds Patty doing her homework. Patty says she is taking cousin Betsy to a dance that night, and since Cathy would prefer to stay home and wash her hair, Patty asks if she can finish her homework for her. Cathy tells Patty that she ought to do it herself. This scene presents both sides of the split perfectly. Cathy is performing the domestic tasks of grocery shopping and putting away products, while Patty—who does not offer to help—asks Cathy to do something dishonest, since she is "just going to stay home anyway." The depiction places the two twins in direct opposition to each other, and even though the episode ends with the cousins reconciling, the oppositions presented in this scene ultimately lead to a conflict within the family. In other words, Patty's desires to leave the home and attend a party—normal activities for a teenager but activities that, from a split perspective, belong on the evil side of the split—create disruption in the harmony of the household.

CAREER INTERESTS

Throughout the series, Patty pursues career interests to earn money for various things that her parents either won't cover or that she doesn't *want* them to cover. Unlike the male characters in these shows, Patty's career pursuits always result in trouble. She is perpetually identified as performing unsuccessfully in the public realm. Cathy is almost never pursuing employment but is most often found doing the housework (without being asked), while Patty is out working, dating, shopping, or attending parties. Consequently, Cathy frequently has to come to Patty's rescue from her career pursuits. For example, in the episode "The Working Girl,"[16] a friend who works for the Shake Shop asks Patty to tell his boss he can't be at work that day because he has to quit the job. Patty asks how much he makes and becomes interested in the position, so she goes to the soda fountain shop to convince the boss to hire her. He says he needs someone with experience. Patty creates a makeshift stage on the counter and uses donuts and cupcakes to act out how many people will be coming in to request her tables; the boss agrees to hire her. She begins working and is doing a good job, but she is quickly exhausted and can't keep up. Martin, however, is so proud of her hard work and determination that he writes an editorial about "good teenagers." Patty had initially decided to quit the job, but after Martin's editorial is published, she feels she can't quit; she doesn't want to be perceived as a quitter (i.e., she doesn't want to disappoint her family because they are so proud of their "working girl"). Patty isn't performing any duties that would have been easier for the previous teen-age-male employee, yet Patty is quickly taught the "lesson" that such pursuits aren't appropriate her. She is depicted as wanting a job but not being able to maintain one because of fatigue, even though the requisite tasks were supposedly no obstacle for her male friend. Even when Cathy's determination to "not be a quitter" should be applauded, the depiction maintains her inability to do the job. Cathy even offers to help Patty by filling in for her one day. This is typical of the good twins, who are always saving the evil twins from themselves and from their own "self-serving" desires.

In the episode "Babysitters,"[17] Patty decides to start her own business. Her motive for earning money, as usual, involves a dance; she wants to buy an expensive dress for the dance in an effort to convince Richard to take her instead of Sue Ellen. She believes Martin will surely pay for it, saying, "I have dad wrapped around my little finger. All I have to say is 'Papa?'" Of course, Martin ultimately says "no" to the dress, but Patty is not deterred. The sensible Cathy replies, "But Patty, your father said you can't have the dress." Manipulating her father's words, Patty says, "Oh, no he didn't. He said when you're old enough to pay for the dress yourself, you're old enough to pick your own dresses." In an effort to satisfy her desires, Patty establishes "Doctor's Babysitter Service" to organize babysitters for families in need. The first day that she establishes her unofficial business, she impulsively agrees to find five babysitters at once for five couples, who all have the same "building meeting" to attend. Patty agrees to do so because her "whole future as a business woman and a wife depend on what happens today." She also claims that "messing up" this gig could result in her being an "old maid." Instead of finding the five babysitters, however, Patty realizes that she can make more profit if she and Richard cover the babysitting themselves. As Patty goes back and forth among apartments, she is depicted as not being able to handle even the smallest of parenting tasks. Cathy eventually arrives, after writing and posting a letter to her father, and finds that everything is in chaos. Patty claims to have declared war. However, the situation calms down when Cathy arrives, and she quickly gets both babies asleep in the nursery. Then, one of the older boys falls asleep, and Richard is the one to pick him up, kiss his cheek, and take him to bed. Eventually, everyone, including Patty and Richard, is asleep, except one troublemaking child named Bobby. Bobby turns up the TV and awakens almost everyone. Cathy comes in and tells Patty to go ahead and leave and she will handle everything, but Patty refuses because she was the "one to get [them] into this mess." In a tone indicating that she hopes Patty has learned her lesson, Cathy replies, "Okay, you're the boss." In the final scene, Patty descends the stairs at home in her new dress, and her father says, "You must have really impressed [Richard] with your business ability to get him to break his date with Sue Ellen and take you out." Patty responds, "I didn't impress him; I put him in a state of shock. He's taking me out because he says I'm helpless without him." Natalie jumps in, saying, "That's a marvelous approach, dear. Remember it." Patty asks, "You mean it's been used before," and Martin answers, "I'm pretty sure Eve asked Adam to pull down the branch so she could reach the apple."

Patty is again depicted as not having the abilities to support her career desires. Just as she was unable to successfully perform her waitressing duties in "The Working Girl," she is unable to perform even the most basic domestic and parenting tasks. Even Richard, who successfully and lovingly puts one young boy in his bed, is depicted as being more adept at these domestic duties than Patty. Cathy, on the other hand, is so skilled in these areas that she is immediately able to save the day. Patty's career interests are incongruous with domesticity, and she stands in opposition to Cathy, who has not only spent the evening at home taking care of family matters (writing a letter to her father) but who also handles the children's needs effortlessly. Here, again, Cathy's ability to prioritize family places her on the good side of the split, while Patty, who is depicted as being selfish, manipulating her father's words to get what she wants and then endangering the safety of children by not providing enough caretakers, appears not to care as much about family. Last, Patty is essentially told that successful career interests do not make her "helpless enough" for boys to be attracted to her, a lesson both of her parents confirm. Thus, Patty is told it is better for her to suppress the desires of independence that belong on the evil side of the split, if she wants boys to like her.

In another episode, Cathy displays a spark of career interest but ultimately realizes that it just isn't for her. The episode "The Actress"[18] presents Patty performing as Cleopatra in *Antony and Cleopatra* at the Brooklyn Heights Theater. Patty's career interests come to the fore almost immediately, when she manipulatively asks her Dad to show her how the printing press at his work functions. Her motive is to write her own good review and print it before the show opens so that it can go into the actual newspaper following her performance. She mails the review anonymously to the paper, but the editor recognizes it right away as the "oldest trick in the book." He likes her initiative, though, and decides to send someone to review the play legitimately. Meanwhile, Cathy is helping Patty with her lines, and Patty begins taking her role as an actress too far, saying to her family, "I just want all of you to know that whatever happens tomorrow night, I'll never forget you." She believes she is going to be a star. As opening night approaches, though, Patty loses her voice. The doctor says that nothing is wrong with her, that her illness is psychosomatic. He believes Patty is too afraid to open in front of the newspaper critic. Since Cathy has been helping Patty with her lines all along, she takes Patty's place in the show. Again, Cathy saves Patty from herself. Cathy begins the performance, but Patty gets her voice back in the middle of the show. Instead of allowing Cathy to finish the show, Patty goes on stage to perform simultaneously with Cathy. Patty has no regard for the production, only for her own performance. The audience begins to laugh when the cousins start swapping Cleopatra's lines back and forth. Eventually, Patty rips the crown off of

Cathy's head, and an audience member asks, "Why doesn't one of them get off the stage?" In the end, a talent scout visits Patty after seeing the play and talks with her about signing a contract for a movie because he thinks she will be a star. Patty immediately loses her voice again.

Patty's determination and hard work are depicted as arrogance. Patty again lacks the ability to fulfill her career interests, while Cathy, who has no real career interests, is able to perform the duties effortlessly. As with other depictions, the qualities that place Cathy on the good side of the split—selflessly helping Patty run lines and being her understudy when needed—allow her to lead a better, more peaceful life, and the qualities that place Patty on the evil side of the split—pursuing fame and working hard for success outside of the home—always get her in trouble and result in her being taught lessons about how she *should* behave.

In the episode "The Songwriters,"[19] Patty is again mad at Richard, so she begins the episode impulsively tearing up his pictures. Natalie consoles her by describing a time when she and Martin broke up; he won her back by writing her a poem. Patty decides to do the same for Richard, but instead of writing it herself, she plagiarizes a poem and gives it to Richard as her own. Everyone is impressed by what they believe are Patty's writing abilities. Then, when Cathy and Patty are watching TV together, the actor/singer Jimmy Dean announces a songwriting contest. The doorbell rings and Patty knows it is her date. Cathy says, "Enjoy yourself." Then, Cathy decides to set Patty's poem to music. When Patty and Richard return, they hear Cathy performing the song she has written to Patty's lyrics. Against Patty's wishes, Richard insists on sending it into the songwriting contest. When Richard asks her about her resistance, she says she "wouldn't want to commercialize their talent." Richard replies, "I don't understand you, Patty. Normally, you have more angles than Sergeant Bilko;[20] but now you've got a chance to win 100 bucks and maybe be famous, and you don't want to invest in a five-cent stamp?" Richard takes the song and says he will mail it for them first thing in the morning. Patty knows she needs to tell Cathy, so she shows Cathy the original poem in the book. Trustingly, Cathy immediately thinks someone has stolen Patty's poem, not the other way around. Patty admits, "Boy, you must really love me. *I* stole the poem." Cathy asks how she did it, and Patty responds, "With my crooked little pencil, that's how." Cathy insists they must tell Richard the truth, but rather than be concerned about getting in serious copyright trouble, Patty asks, "Have you ever seen Sue Ellen on ice skates? If he takes her ice skating, I'm sunk." In the end, the song wins the contest and is performed by Jimmy Dean in front of a television audience of millions. Charles Worth Remington, the actual author of the poem, contacts the girls to thank them because his "long-lost love" saw the show, recognized his poem, and reunited with him.

Patty is depicted as preferring to be dishonest to satisfy her desires, rather than rely on ability. Again, she desires the fame and success but does not possess the talents to achieve her "dreams." Also, Patty's efforts are depicted as being excessively self-serving. Even once she has realized the trouble she has caused and comes clean to Cathy, her only fear is losing Richard again. As usual, Cathy is presented as having the talent but never wanting/needing to use it because she understands the consequences of self-serving actions—a reason she, versus Patty, chooses the good life. Even though Patty is cunning in almost every episode, Cathy is depicted here as always wanting to see the best in her (e.g., believing the actual author of the poem plagiarized Patty). Patty's desires to pursue things outside of the home—this time poetry and romance—result in her realization that it is better to be more like Cathy.

In another episode, Patty establishes another business. In "The Horoscope,"[21] Ross is reading a book about astrology at the breakfast table. Patty sees it and becomes interested in the subject. As usual, Patty needs money, even though this time, it is in order to buy her mom a birthday present. Since Cathy will not let her borrow money—because she doesn't think it is good for her—Patty decides to develop a fortune-telling business, making 25 cents on every prediction. She reads horoscopes and uses astrology to give advice, and eventually, many students come to her for predictions. Eventually, she can't keep up with business, so she asks Cathy to join her because "two people can make more than one." Then, a detective shows up about an "illegal fortune teller" operating in the neighborhood, and Patty is forced to shut down her business. In the end, the predictions she had made for friends all begin to go wrong, and she realizes her business plan was not a good one.

Much like her depiction in "Working Girl" and "Babysitters," Patty is depicted as needing to use deceit in order to pursue career opportunities. In this episode, she is not only portrayed as being intentionally deceitful to make money; the episode also continues the pattern of Patty not having the ability to perform the tasks required for continued employment. Patty cleverly and independently finds a solution to her money problem, but as with other examples, those qualities are depicted as flaws, as leading to her downfall. Cathy is portrayed not only as having the good sense to want to teach Patty to save her money (e.g., not letting her borrow money), but also as coming to Patty's rescue again when she is unable to perform successfully in the public realm.

Finally, in the episode "The Tycoons,"[22] Cathy sews a dress from scratch (a further example of her domestic prowess) that features a polka dotted cat on the front. Patty sees it and thinks it looks awful, asking, "Are you sure you are going to like wearing something nobody else is wearing?" At school, girls begin to swarm Cathy, asking where she bought the dress. When she tells them she made it, Patty starts taking orders from the girls for more dresses in any color they choose. At the end of the day, Patty wants to start a partnership with Cathy because she already has orders for over 40 dresses sold at $9.95 each. Thinking logistically, Cathy says it took her three days to make her own dress, and she doesn't know how she could be expected to make over 40 by Monday, which is the unrealistic timeline promised by Patty to customers. Patty says, "You're the creative genius and I'm the business genius; together, we are going to build an empire. Do you know how many people built careers in one little thing? Bolton created one little steamboat. Whitney created one little cotton gin. The Wright brothers . . ." Cathy interrupts, claiming, "Patty, you don't know anything about dresses," but Patty believes she can learn. She develops the Worldwide

Dress Company and sends a telegram to one of the best fashion designers (Gregory Madison), requesting a meeting about "a matter of mutual financial interest." The designer assumes they are a new company, run by males, so he tells the secretary to get a box of very good cigars—something to appeal to businessmen. Patty and Cathy meet with him as President and Vice President of the Worldwide Dress Company, and Patty proceeds to pitch him to buy in to the company. Mr. Madison agrees to fund supplies, and Patty forms a board of directors for the company, tells Cathy to get to work, and later, agrees to supply a local department store with 244 dresses in three days. While a frustrated Cathy feverishly attempts to meet these sewing demands, Patty is off going to the movies or ice skating. In the end, they get a visit from the IRS and realize they can't make a profit *and* pay taxes.

As with the "Babysitters," "Songwriters," and "Actress" episodes, Patty's career pursuits are depicted as needing the talents of others, mainly Cathy, to become realities. Patty's grit is rarely recognized as such; instead, her resolve ends up being interpreted as greedy, unpredictable, unrealistic, and ultimately, abusive to others; episodes depict potentially good traits for an independent teenager as evil traits that lead to trouble. Like other examples of the good twins, Cathy is the quintessential voice of reason, claiming, "This isn't a good idea" or asking, "Shouldn't we think about this?" Patty's sense of purpose is undermined by the show's need to portray her as impulsive, a quality that more effectively places her on the evil side of the split.

POLITICAL INTERESTS

The category of political interests includes the desire to be elected to a position, to campaign for a cause, or to be appointed to a leadership role. In the episode "The President,"[23] Patty is chosen as a candidate for the president of the Girls' League position, but Patty is confused because she had nominated Cathy, who is also in the running. The girls do not want to run against each other, so they decide over dinner to withdraw, but the parents convince them that doing so would undermine the entire political system of their country. Martin says, "If both of you have been accepted as nominees, neither one of you can withdraw. Politics is a healthy form of competition." Patty and Cathy discuss running in the election, and Patty says, "They need someone like you to run." Cathy replies, "I would be selfish if I ran because your being president would be good for the League and good for you. It might give you a sense of responsibility." Patty is offended by that statement and admits that she was also trying to be unselfish when she nominated Cathy, because she was hoping it would make her socialize more with boys. Now, Cathy is offended, so they both get mad and decide to run against each other. When Cathy gives her first campaign speech, she says, "I'm not much of a politician. If you are looking for someone who can do the Bossa Nova and the Baked Potato, vote for Patty. But if you want someone who isn't flighty, who will devote herself to the tasks at hand with dignity, then I ask that you vote for me." Patty then makes her speech, saying, "At least I know the difference between the mashed potato and the baked potato; one is a dance and one is a vegetable." Everyone laughs. "If you want a program of chess and classical concerts, elect her. But if you want a program of fun, elect me." As they continue to campaign, Patty reveals that she is running on a platform that advocates for more student dances and more freedom in choices of school attire, while Cathy is advocating more guest speakers and a better curriculum. The girls become so competitive that, in the end, they both lose, and the third nominee, who did not campaign at all, wins the election.

Since both girls seem to display political interests in this episode, it is important to look at how each of those interests is depicted regarding the good/evil split. First, Patty's reason for nominating Cathy is so she can socialize more with boys, and her reasons for wanting to be elected is to hold more student dances and require more fashion freedom. Cathy's reason for nominating Patty is so she can become more responsible, and her reasons for wanting to be elected is to present more guest speakers and improve the curriculum. The episode maintains the good/evil split, even though both are interested in serving in leadership roles. Patty's reasons are depicted as childish and selfish, while Cathy's reasons are sound. We see a similar treatment in other series. For example, in *Bewitched*, Samantha campaigns for a new stop sign to keep children safe, which could be interpreted as a political/civic interest, but her interests are portrayed as differing drastically from Serena's, which involve coordinating a protest/sit-in that gets her arrested. Second, as the episode proceeds, Cathy takes on more and more of Patty's competitive spirit. Consequently, when both girls lose in the end to a nominee who did not even attempt to compete, the drive and intensity displayed by the girls are interpreted as flaws, as qualities that ultimately lead to their downfall.

Another episode that puts the cousins in competition with each other (because they are "foolishly" attempting to function in the public sphere) is "The Little Dictator."[24] Mr. Brewster, the school principal, is set to choose a student who will act as the principal for a week. Patty and Cathy are up against each other for the job. Mr. Brewster chooses Cathy and calls Patty into his office to notify her. Upset with the decision, Patty shows little self-control in handling the decision. Cathy's first task as principal is to teach the chemistry class, but Patty attempts to sabotage her efforts by belittling her and making jokes throughout the period. When she ignores Cathy's warnings, Patty is given three demerits. Later, an angry Patty draws a line down their bedroom so they can each stay on their own side; she doesn't want to share anything with Cathy because she is jealous of her new leadership role. In order to make Patty understand the difficulties of leading, Cathy asks Patty to teach history for her that day. Initially, her classmates cheer for Patty, but when she attempts to get any work accomplished, they make jokes. She, too, ends up giving her classmates demerits, including giving ten demerits to Richard after he insists on performing a magic show for the class. That evening, Patty is worried that Richard will break up with her, but when he comes over, he tells her he is proud of her, saying, "You had a job, and you did it." Patty is relieved and leaves to help Richard with his homework.

Similar to "The President," both cousins desire a leadership role but are depicted as doing so for very different reasons and with very different approaches. And whereas Patty expects Richard to treat her the same way she treated Cathy following the demerits, he treats her with respect; thus, the episode ends without Patty making any apology to Cathy. When the cousins are placed in similar situations—campaigning for an election or serving as a principal—each one desires to be successful. However, Patty's methods to achieve success are repeatedly depicted as self-serving, and Cathy's methods persistently function to serve others, thus consistently maintaining the split dynamic.

ASSERTIVENESS

The quality of assertiveness is included on the evil side of the split because it is typically depicted as a desire for control or power, rather than merely signifying confidence. Regarding the good twins, they are often portrayed as confident within the home, but evil twins are depicted as needing to control their worlds outside of the home. In other series, assertiveness is most often seen when evil twins try to seduce men, single or married. This does not happen as often in *The Patty Duke Show*, but Patty does occasionally try to steal boys away from Cathy. More often, Patty is portrayed as needing to take control of a situation to get what she wants. In the episode, "The Conquering Hero,"[25] Patty, who is a cheerleader for the basketball team, is upset because the star player of the Brooklyn Heights team, Stretch Edwards, is supposed to move to another school with his parents' job relocation before he can play in the championship game. Patty tells Martin, and he is upset that no one offered a home for Stretch until the finish of the championship. Patty asks if he would have offered, had he known about the relocation. Martin says he would have, and Patty runs to the front door to bring in Stretch and all of his bags. Stretch's needs go beyond having meals prepared and clothes cleaned, though—all tasks performed by Natalie and Cathy, even though the decision was made by Patty and Martin. Eventually, Stretch discovers that he is failing a class, and the cousins intervene to tutor him so he can pass the course and play the game. Even though Patty has been assertive in saving the fate of the basketball team, she is depicted as being conniving and inconsiderate. Once Patty gets her way, she displays no regret for having tricked her father into supporting a star basketball player through the end of the season, and Martin displays no surprise that she has succeeded. The needs of Patty's family always come second to her own desires. Even though one could argue that any teenager in Patty's situation would know her family has the room and resources to support a student and that her assertiveness in offering her place was a thoughtful gesture, her actions are depicted as ultimately self-serving.

"The Princess Cathy"[26] is a unique episode because it portrays a boy choosing Cathy over Patty. In the beginning, Patty and Cathy are fighting over a new boy from India named Kalmere (Richard Caruso), whom they assume is an orphan because he claims to live in a house with 50 people and to have never touched money before. When Kalmere comes over to see Cathy, Patty keeps trying to steal him away. Eventually, Patty walks him home, even though she can see Cathy likes him and is visibly upset. Patty replies to Cathy, "This is a free country, and he isn't your type anyway." When Cathy asks why Patty was throwing herself at him, Patty says, "He needs someone who can teach him about American cultures, and I'm as American as apple pie." Cathy asks, "Then what am I," and Patty answers, "A wet crumpet."

Most of the boys included in the series want to date Patty, who is more popular, outgoing, and trendy. At first, it seems surprising that such a handsome boy prefers Cathy, but the episode soon begins to indicate why Cathy is the perfect choice for Kalmere's situation. Kalmere has traveled to America specifically to find a wife, and according to the split theory, women on the evil side of the split do not make good wives. At one point, Cathy and Kalmere are discussing their individual dreams; when asked what her dream is, Cathy answers, "Oh, to make a chocolate soufflé that doesn't fall." Her dream in life does not exist outside of the home or even the kitchen—a dream that would be in line with the expectations of many boys looking for wives in this decade. When Kalmere proposes to Cathy, she initially agrees, until she is made aware that he will be encouraged to have many wives. She then declines. With the introduction of a potential marriage, this episode brings the split unambiguously into view. Patty spends most of the episode being depicted as a man-stealer, as are most of the other alter egos in this study, and Cathy is depicted as a domestic goddess, dreaming of perfect kitchen creations in her future.

Finally, Patty is often depicted as asserting herself, not to achieve something she necessarily wants but to keep something from others, mainly Cathy. For example, in "Patty, the Foster Mother,"[27] the cousins' class at school is adopting a young child from Korea, which means they will be responsible for gathering donations and supplies to send to the orphan. One student has to volunteer to serve as the foster "parent"—a person who will be in charge of the initiative—and Cathy clearly wants to serve in this role. Upon seeing this, however, Patty insists to the class that it should be her. When it comes to domesticity, Cathy is always depicted as being in her comfort zone. Whether she is caring for many children, as she does in "Babysitters," or putting away groceries, as she does in "The Perfect Hostess," Cathy is an obvious choice for a project that involves making good decisions regarding the needs of a child. This is not a task Patty would enjoy, yet the portrayal indicates that the mere appeal of beating Cathy at something supersedes her typical distaste and ineptitude regarding parenting.

CONCLUSIONS

Patty's main flaw as the evil twin to Cathy's good twin is her desire to dominate the public sphere, which grinds against social norms and always ends in trouble. Cathy may have previously traveled the world with her father, the foreign correspondent, but in every episode, Cathy reminds us that home is really where she wants to be. Cathy's depictions almost always align her with domesticity, whether she is washing dishes, cleaning the bedroom, or putting away groceries. Even when Patty has duties, such as homework, that serve to tether her to the domestic sphere, she attempts to delegate those tasks to Cathy, since she [Cathy] doesn't "want to go out anyway." Depictions of Cathy as easily content and Patty as perpetually restless program the young female viewer to feel comfortable with the idea of one side of the split and uncomfortable with the other side. These depictions serve to show her what she *ought* to be and what she ought *not* to be.

Just as Cathy trades her life of travel for a simpler, more normal one in Brooklyn Heights, Samantha Stephens swears off her magical powers for the chosen life of an average housewife in *Bewitched*. Sacrifice and forbearance are at the core of Cathy's and Samantha's characters, in addition to their affinities for the domestic space, while selfishness and impulsiveness, in addition to their need to function in the public space, serve to connect Patty with Serena.

NOTES

1. *The Patty Duke Show*, season 2, episode 18, "The Perfect Hostess," written by Arnold Horwitt, directed by Don Weis, January 1965.

2. On a serious note, Marilyn Monroe (Norma Jean) had a troubled childhood that involved her mother being clinically diagnosed with schizophrenia and with Norma being orphaned. I do not mean to minimize the trauma of these experiences, and I have always admired Monroe's strength, kindness, and resilience throughout her life.

3. Sheldon, *The Other Side of Me*, 210.

4. This interview can be viewed at the following link: https://www.youtube.com/watch?v=Y5s4M5Kx6yI.

5. This interview can be viewed at the following link: https://www.youtube.com/watch?v=WrbgHj0bAL4.

6. Sheldon, *The Other Side of Me*, 210.

7. In addition to claiming "it was as though [he] were on a date with 2 different people," when discussing Marilyn Monroe, Sheldon also admitted to creating *The Patty Duke Show* to capture the two sides of Patty Duke. In other words, his perception of women and multiple identities goes further than merely one example.

8. In 1955, Monroe gave an interview with Ed Murrow on the television program *Person to Person*. Murrow asked her if she had been on the cover of every magazine. She said, "no." He asked if there was a magazine cover that she wished she had been on. She replied that she always wanted to be on the cover of *Ladies Home Journal*, but she was always asked to do the covers of men's magazines. One must wonder why she wouldn't be on the cover of *Ladies Home Journal*, considering her fame at the time, but this likely has something to do with her role as a sex symbol and the type of female audience *Ladies Home Journal* sought to entice. Later, Monroe was asked if she is good in the kitchen and makes her own bed each day. Monroe very awkwardly answers the questions, but it takes many questions such as these before

Monroe is asked about her new production company and upcoming films. This interview can be viewed at the following link: https://www.youtube.com/watch?v=L05TYBXwU3A.

9. These are lyrics from the title song of *The Patty Duke Show*, written by Sid Ramer.

10. *The Patty Duke Show*, season 1, episode 3, "The Elopement," written by Sheldon, directed by Asher, October 1963.

11. *The Patty Duke Show*, season 1, episode 4, "The House Guest," written by Sheldon, directed by Asher, October 1963.

12. *The Patty Duke Show*, season 1, episode 10, "Double Date," written by Rick Singer and Dick Chevillat, directed by Stanley Prager, November 1963.

13. *The Patty Duke Show*, season 1, episode 12, "How to Be Popular," written by Sydney Sheldon, directed by William Asher, December 1963.

14. It is also possible that Richard's assessment that Cathy is "anti-boy" was a comment on public ideals in the sixties regarding feminism and lesbianism. If Cathy is deemed as not wanting to dance with a boy, rather than assuming she just wants to dance alone, her contemporary surroundings assume she must be "anti-boy" or must prefer women to men.

15. *The Patty Duke Show*, season 1, episode 6, "Slumber Party," written by Pauline and Leo Townsend, directed by Stanley Prager, October 1963.

16. *The Patty Duke Show*, season 1, episode 35, "The Working Girl," written by Sydney Sheldon, directed by Stanley Prager, May 1964.

17. *The Patty Duke Show*, season 1, episode 7, "The Babysitters," written by R.S. Allen, directed by Stanley Prager, October 1963.

18. *The Patty Duke Show*, season 1, episode 11, "The Actress," written by Sydney Sheldon, directed by Stanley Prager, November1963.

19. *The Patty Duke Show*, season 1, episode 13, "The Songwriters," written by Sydney Sheldon, directed by William Asher, December 1963.

20. This is a reference to the *Phil Silvers Show* that begin airing in 1955. Silvers stars as Master Sergeant Ernest G. Bilko of the U.S. Army and spends most of his time getting other people to do work for him or participate in his get-rich-quick schemes.

21. *The Patty Duke Show*, season 1, episode 17, "Horoscope," written by Sydney Sheldon, directed by Alan Rafkin, January 1964.

22. *The Patty Duke Show*, season 1, episode 18, "The Tycoons," written by Sydney Sheldon, directed by Alan Rafkin, January 1964.

23. *The Patty Duke Show*, season 1, episode 9, "The President," written by Sydney Sheldon, directed by Stanley Prager, November 1963.

24. *The Patty Duke Show*, season 1, episode 34, "The Little Dictator," written by Sydney Sheldon, directed by Stanley Prager, May 1964.

25. *The Patty Duke Show*, season 1, episode 8, "The Conquering Hero," written by Jerry David and Lee Loeb, directed by Asher, November 1963. Jerry David also wrote episodes for *Bewitched*.

26. *The Patty Duke Show*, season 1, episode 14, "The Princess Cathy," written by Sydney Sheldon, directed by Stanley Prager, December 1963.

27. *The Patty Duke Show*, season 1, episode 31, "Patty, the Foster Mother," written by Sydney Sheldon, directed by Stanley Prager, April 1964.

2

Bewitched

After directing nine episodes of *The Patty Duke Show* in its first season, with his final season-one episode occurring in May of 1964, William Asher began directing another production that coincidentally, just like *The Patty Duke Show*, featured twins: *Bewitched*. The series was created by Sol Saks, who previously and subsequently worked with Sherwood Schwartz, creator of *Gilligan's Island* and *The Brady Bunch*. Saks wrote only the pilot episode and claimed the concept was based on ideas from the films *I Married a Witch*[1] and *Bell, Book, and Candle*.[2] Both films involve witches marrying mortals, and their influences on *Bewitched* are clear. Airing in September of 1964, *Bewitched* soared to the top of the Nielsen ratings in its first season and ran for 254 episodes in the span of eight years. The show starred Elizabeth Montgomery as Samantha, a witch who has chosen to marry a mortal, Darrin Stephens (Dick York and Dick Sergeant), and live the life of a housewife.

Even the weekly animated introductory segment[3] worked to underscore the "this or that" depiction of women in the sixties. In the famous intro, Samantha flies through the sky on a broom, wearing a black witch's dress, cape, and hat. Once she lands in the home, though, she removes her witch's hat and holds it out in her hand. She twitches her nose, and the hat becomes a frying pan, her witch outfit becomes a blue dress and white apron, and the change results in Darrin kissing her on the cheek. She transforms from witch to housewife once she transfers from public to private sphere.

Montgomery also portrays Samantha's evil identical cousin, Serena, by wearing a dark wig in most episodes, flashy clothes, and an everchanging beauty mark.[4] Montgomery was clearly an influential cog in the wheel, and her influence may have something to do with the fact that *Bewitched* used a remarkable number of female television writers, compared to other examples from the 1960s.[5] Of the 254 *Bewitched* episodes, thirty-four are written or co-written by women, representing

Figure 2.1.   Elizabeth Montgomery as Samantha in *Bewitched,*
AF Archive / Alamy Stock Photo

about 13.38 percent of the series—the highest percentage of all shows analyzed in this study—and of the twenty-two evil-twin episodes, five are written or co-written by women, representing roughly 14.2 percent of those episodes.

Following 1950s television, where scholars argue that mothers were marginalized and devalued by being removed from scenes to perform housework, while the important familial discussion occur among the men and boys,[6] the 1960s introduced sitcoms with witches and genies—women with supernatural abilities—inspiring scholars to conclude that these characters embodied women's emerging social and sexual power in the sixties.[7] In discussing fifties television, Leibman found that television worked to "re-channel careerist desires [in women] by extolling the virtues of being a good wife and mother."[8] Leibman goes on to argue that the combination of these representations and the television advertisements served to show women what they ought to be—to create the happy housewife consumer. I argue that television producers are attempting to program viewers in the same way—to re-channel desires involving independence—vis-à-vis the evil-twin characters of these shows. On the one hand, we have the Samanthas, Jeannies, Cathys, and Alices of these sitcoms, extolling the virtues of homemaking through happy depictions of housework and service—just as their fifties counterparts did—while on the other hand, we have the Serenas, Sister Jeannies, Pattys, and Emmas embodying the consequences of independence—showing female viewers that independence leaves them unhappy, petty, jealous, unfulfilled, unaccepted, and ultimately, countercultural. These depictions—the happy housewife and the evil twin—are serving the same purpose: to create the happy housewife consumer, who buys products not just for herself but for an entire family. If we are to subscribe to Hall's theory that representation communicates what a society thinks of itself, that signifying practice "makes things mean,"[9] then the message is clear: female dependence is good and female independence is bad—both for consumerism and the greater good of American society.

Before moving into the categories identified by Friedan of the evil side of the split, I'd like to address the ways in which the show, in general, worked to establish the split, providing early depictions of the identical cousins as completely oppositional. The first episode that includes Samantha's evil-twin cousin, Serena, is "And Then There Were Three."[10] This episode establishes that all qualities belonging to motherhood and wifehood shall not only be performed happily and effortlessly by Samantha, they are qualities that lie entirely beyond the parameters of Serena's understanding. In this episode, Samantha is in the hospital, having just given birth to Tabitha, and Serena appears sporting short black hair, wearing a long black fur coat, gloves, and purse, and smoking a long cigarette. She stands in complete contrast to Samantha, who is wearing a soft pink, lacy nightgown. Serena says she would like to leave something for the baby, but her idea for a gift is "a centaur." Samantha replies, "Serena, there's something you should know; I married a mortal, so if you still want to get her something, how about buying her a rattle?" Serena says, "That's brilliant! I never would have thought of that," and Samantha replies that it takes practice. Still attempting to be thoughtful, Serena fills the hospital room completely with fresh flowers. Samantha says, "I don't mean to seem ungrateful, but they have a rule about filling the room with too many flowers. In fact, you're not even supposed to be here." Serena acknowledges that a nurse tried to stop her from coming in, but she handled it by turning the nurse into a frog and sticking the frog in her purse.

At the moment that Samantha becomes the full embodiment of the good side of the split—being now both wife and mother—the character Serena is introduced. Serena is not only depicted as having no idea what to buy a baby, but she is also portrayed as not even understanding the hospital rules regarding new moms—a position that depicts her presence as harmful to the situation, something that could be argued about the public perception of feminism to motherhood. Everything pertaining to motherhood is beyond Serena's understanding. Additionally, Serena makes it clear that motherhood is not something she is interested in seeking. In "Cousin Serena Strikes Again, Part 2,"[11] Serena reverses her spell on someone, and Samantha thanks her for doing the right thing. Then, Samantha says to Serena, "You'd better get back to watching Tabitha now." Clearly irritated, Serena asks, "Cuz, how much longer do I have to babysit Tabitha?" Samantha answers, "Not long and don't worry. I'll do the same for you one day." Serena expresses her intense rejection of domesticity and motherhood by replying, "I sincerely hope not!"

These divisions extend to housekeeping as well. The episode "Marriage, Witch's Style"[12] opens with Samantha baking a cake. Serena appears in a long tiger fur coat and mentions her recent adventures, which Samantha admits sound like fun. Serena says, "Oh, I'm bored with fun. There must be something more to life than happiness. Well, there's heartache. Oh, I would just love to have an aching heart for a change,

Figure 2.2. Montgomery as Serena and Erin Murphy as Tabitha in "Samantha and the Troll," *Bewitched,* **Archive PL / Alamy Stock Photo**

like you." Samantha asks, "Who's aching?" Serena replies, "Oh, the grubby little housewife role can't be all fun." Serena decides she wants to experiment with dating a mortal, and she eventually desires to invite her new mortal over for dinner with Samantha and Darrin. When she uses witchcraft to conjure up the meal, though, Samantha makes it disappear. Serena asks, "What's the matter? Chateau Brillion too well done?" Samantha says, "Everything is too well done. Come with me. Here are the recipes; here's the food; here's the heat. Now start cooking." Astonished, Serena responds, "Me? I don't even know how to boil water. Oh, come on, Cuz. Let me whip up a little gourmet meal." Samantha insists, "If you're going to marry a mortal, you are going to have to learn to live like one. Mortals are uncomfortable with per-fection. They absolutely love helpless women, so a little imperfection in your dinner can only endear yourself to him." Naturally, Serena cringes at the word "helpless"—a scene that reminds us of *The Patty Duke* scene when Patty's parents remind her that men love helpless women. Samantha exerts extra effort to do things as men prefer, while Serena has no knowledge of or desire for cooking or service. Samantha under-stands the need for men to feel their wives need them and is happy to play into that, if it makes her husband happy, while Serena has no desire to pretend to be helpless to attract a mortal; and ultimately, Samantha is fulfilled, while Serena is bored.

Boredom is a topic that is at the heart of *The Feminine Mystique*, as I've stated elsewhere:

> Friedan described what she called the "problem that has no name"—the widespread boredom and restlessness housewives were experiencing in the 1950s and 60s. Many of these white middle-class housewives had been educated alongside the men but had given up their professional dreams for the promise of ultimate feminine fulfillment; women believed in this promise and found themselves bewildered by the actual boredom of homemaking. They had listened to the television shows of the fifties and early sixties, such as the *Leave it to Beaver* episode "Beaver's IQ" (1960) when Beaver says, "Girls have it lucky . . . they don't have to be smart; they don't have to get jobs or anything; all they got to do is get married." But after years of dirty diapers, bologna sandwiches, and PTA meetings, these women didn't feel so "lucky." And in the sixties, the "problem that has no name," the actual unhappiness of the American housewife, was finally being discussed.[13]

To support the assertion that these visual texts were in conversation with Friedan, it is significant that *Bewitched* addresses the issue of housewife boredom in multiple episodes. The episode "Mixed Doubles"[14] seems to confirm outright that television writers were creating dialogue that acknowledged the influence of Friedan's theories. The episode opens with Samantha and Darrin in bed reading books. Samantha is reading a book called *Marital Unrest*, and Darrin asks, "Marital unrest? Why'd you buy a book about that?" Samantha answers, "I didn't; Louise Tate insisted upon lending it to me. She says it reveals what you and I are in for. It's about boredom in marriage." Darrin responds, "Sam, in our marriage, boredom will never be a prob-lem." Samantha says, "The author says after several years of marriage, it's common for husbands and wives to feel they'd rather be married to somebody else," and Dar-rin asks, "What does he recommend, therapeutic divorce?" Samantha answers, "Not in chapter one; he merely describes the problem"—a statement that seems to clearly reference Friedan's "problem that has no name." Other examples include the episode "Fastest Gun on Madison Avenue" (1966),[15] when Samantha tells Darrin, "You know there's a lot more to running a house than most people think." Darrin replies, "Honey, I think it's wonderful the way you've adjusted," and Samantha claims, "I love being a housewife." Darrin then asks, "Are you sure you won't get bored once the novelty has worn off?" Confidently, Samantha says, "How could I be bored being married to someone like you?" Lest viewers speculate that Samantha misses her life before swearing off witchcraft to be a wife, the show persistently reminds us that Samantha is the happy one, and Serena remains unfulfilled.

This dynamic is galvanized by the episode "Chance on Love."[16] Samantha arrives with groceries, and a hidden Serena begins magically placing the products in cabinets. Samantha asks, "Okay, who's the wise witch?" Serena appears and says, "Wiser than you are cousin, drudging around the kitchen like a slave." Samantha defends her existence, saying, "Serena, doing housework is one of the joys of living the mortal life. It means you are doing something for someone you love." Later in the episode, the dual identities of American women are revealed explicitly. As a favor to Samantha, Serena is posing as her to sell raffle tickets, when a rich young man, George, says he wants to buy all of her tickets. They go to dinner together, and later when he appears at the Stephens' house, Serena tries to explain how she is Serena, not Samantha. George responds, "Oh, sure, sure. You're Samantha when you are in suburbia, but you are Serena when you are out on the town." His dialogue articulates the this or that/good or evil dynamic applied to depictions of women.

The episode "The Corsican Cousins"[17] expresses a similar sentiment regarding the assumed boredom of housewifery. Samantha's mother, Endora (Agnes Moorehead), asks her, "Why don't you take some advice from your cousin Serena. She is quicksilver. She lives in the sparkle of a star and a flash of color." They both see Serena on television wearing a black dress and black feather boa and dancing wildly with two men. Endora asks, "See all the fun you're missing?" Samantha replies, "I wouldn't trade Darrin for a hundred of them," and she leaves. In an attempt to encourage Samantha to think more about herself and less about her husband, Endora says to herself, "There must be some way to remind her of what she has given up." In each situation, the cousins stand in complete opposition: one is depicted as finding joy in service and dependence and feeling fulfilled in a state of selflessness, while the other is portrayed as finding excitement in adventure and independence and feeling unfulfilled in a state of selfishness.

Selfishness is addressed explicitly once Samantha becomes a mother. In "Mrs. Stephens, Where Are You,"[18] Darrin is away on business, and Samantha's mother-in-law, Phyllis Stephens (Mabel Albertson), arrives unannounced to keep her company while he is gone. Serena answers the door and explains that she is Samantha's cousin. Phyllis asks about her granddaughter Tabitha (Erin Murphy) and says she will go upstairs to see her. Serena points to a very large hourglass and says, "not now; her nap still has some time to go." Phyllis responds, "Well, Samantha is trying to keep this baby all to herself, and I think she is being very selfish. Someone other than her mother-in-law should advise her." Serena asks, "For her own good?" "Yes, and for Tabitha's. Why, it would break my heart to see that girl grow up to be just like her mother—selfish." This episode will be discussed at length in the fifth chapter, but it is worth noting here that it was co-written by a female writer, Peggy Chantler Dick—a significant detail considering "selfish" is the quality Phyllis chooses first, when reflecting upon the type of woman she doesn't want her granddaughter to be.

Finally, in general, when she isn't in the mortal world, Serena's surroundings are depicted in a way that is reminiscent of hell. For example, in "Sam and the Hot Bed Warmer," witches are shown gathering on their own turf. Their environment has a red background, a smattering of barren trees, dead moss, and rocks—devoid of natural life—and an abundance of smoke (indicating the fires of hell). This scene is similar to others, such as that in "The Corsican Cousins," when Serena is dancing wildly on the television. Her environment is also red and filled with smoke. If Serena's "home" is akin to hell, the series works to align Serena directly with the quality of evil. In this handful of episodes alone, *Bewitched* references the split, the drudgery of housework, the "problem that has no name," and the ways in which sixties popular culture attempted to associate housewifery with fulfillment—all major themes of Friedan's work. Thus, the series indicates both that the writers were aware of the claims put forward by Friedan and that the influence of *The Feminine Mystique* was substantial and far-reaching. Ultimately, it is worth noting that in all examples, it is both men and women who act affronted when the evil sister/cousin transgresses established order, thus conveying the message that anyone, male or female, may act as measures of social norms and scorn those belonging to the counterculture.

LOOSE INHIBITIONS

Like other shows, *Bewitched* typically depicts qualities of self-interest and independence as selfishness in the evil-twin characters. As Serena explores her own personal interests in things like sexual desire, she is portrayed as being excessively selfish and lacking self-control, rather than merely desiring a sense of separate self—desiring an opportunity to pursue her own interests. Furthermore, as single women, the alter egos are often attempting to seduce men and, at times, steal them away from other women, an activity that conveys the message that single women are unhappy and dissatisfied, while married women are content and fulfilled.

Bewitched reflects these ideas in Serena, and many episodes depict her as embodying Friedan's evil of independence through qualities of sexual excess. In the episode "Darrin on a Pedestal,"[19] even Samantha equates her cousin's self-service with evil. Serena is visiting the "Fisherman's Memorial," when she realizes the statue of the fisherman is very attractive. She zaps the fisherman to life and begins kissing him passionately. She then zaps Darrin into the fisherman's place as the statue. In an effort to serve her own sexual desires, Serena continues to ask the fisherman to lie down with her. She rubs his back, and when he says, "lower," she says, "gladly." Later, Serena and her fisherman are in a restaurant, where they have had too much to drink and are singing loudly. In response to what her cousin is doing, Samantha says, "I have a cousin who makes Lucrezia Borgia look like Shirley Temple." Considering Lucrezia Borgia is often regarded as the quintessential "femme fatale," this statement underscores the treatment of Serena's sexual desires and life of excess as "evil."[20] In this example, the evil woman draws her stolen man into a public venue and puts herself/them on display—not the actions of a demure housewife. In "Samantha Goes South for a Spell,"[21] Samantha leaves the house while Darrin is still sleeping. Serena appears in a black wig and bright pink dress, and she has a black bird on her shoulder. She sneaks into the living room, asking, "Yoohoo, anybody home?" Darrin calls down for Samantha and asks her to fix him an omelet. Serena says, "Oh, this is going to be a riot." She transforms herself into Samantha, and when Darrin comes downstairs, Serena (as Samantha) kisses him passionately. Samantha walks in the front door because she has forgotten her grocery list, sees the kissing, and says, "Hello, Serena." In "Samantha's Hot Bedwarmer,"[22] Serena appears with Samantha and Darrin, while they are on a trip, but she says she can't stay long because "she has to get back before the maharaja's wives return," indicating she is having an adulterous relationship with the Indian prince. The episode "Serena Stops the Show"[23] presents Samantha cooking beef stew for a dinner event including Serena and Larry Tate (David White). Once Larry and Darrin arrive, Serena immediately begins trying to seduce a married Larry by sipping his drink and saying, "your baby blues really turn me on." Samantha quickly replies, "Serena, will you knock it off?" Serena says, "A girl's gotta have some kicks," and Samantha replies, "Do your kicking elsewhere." Serena attempts to flirt often with Larry, as she does again in "Serena's Youth Pill."[24] Serena is alone at the Stephens' home when the doorbell rings. She answers it, sees Larry, and says, "Hi, anything I can do for you?" Larry nervously says "no," claiming that he was just trying to return Darrin's putter. Before he can leave, Serena begins flirting, asking, "Do you know that your far-out, baby-blue eyes kind of turn me on?" Larry responds, "Serena, you certainly know how to flatter the senior citizens," and Serena flirtatiously replies, "Oh, daddy bear; Did I ever tell you that I am simply wild about gray hair? Oh, and I love your sense of humor. So why don't you stick around, and we'll break out a bottle of the bubbly and drink and dance and putter around?" Larry says, "Watch it, Serena. You're gonna turn this old gray fox into the red devil of yesteryear." "And I could do it too," Serena insists. In "Cousin Serena Strikes Again Part 2,"[25] Serena arrives wearing an Egyptian dress, with one side off the shoulder. Samantha asks her to stay, and Darrin angrily insists to Serena, "But for Pete's sake, will you put some clothes on," indicating her attire is sexier than he deems appropriate. Finally, in "Chance on Love,"[26] Samantha comes downstairs in the middle of the night to call for Serena. Serena appears in her party clothes and jewelry, holding an enormous glass of wine. Samantha gives her a look, and Serena responds, "Innocence is not my bag," acknowledging her affinity for bad behavior.

In addition to sexual excess, Serena's loose inhibitions are often depicted as a general lack of self-control, which ranges from her making threats to impulsively turning people into animals (as she does in the very first episode that features her, when she turns the nurse into a frog). For example, in "Cousin Serena Strikes Again Part 1," Clio Vanita (Nancy Kovack) is a very attractive wine producer looking to hire Darrin to design her ads. She attends dinner at the Stephens' house, and Serena, who is there to help, takes over Samantha's voice, speaking for her and often finishing her sentences. At dinner, Clio is very flirtatious with Darrin and says, "I prefer your American men," and Serena (as Samantha) replies, "Just remember, they are *our* American men. Señorita, you haven't even touched your dessert." Clio claims she must always watch her weight, but Larry tells her she has a beautiful figure. Serena (as Samantha) adds, "For an older woman." Later, Clio begins making moves on Darrin in the back yard, but Serena is there to stop her, saying, "No one makes a monkey out of my cousin. In fact, I think my cousin's cousin is going to make a monkey out of you." Serena turns Clio into a monkey, and when Samantha enters and asks what she is doing, Serena calls her own actions, "Good deeds for you, Cuz." Serena has a penchant for turning people into animals when she doesn't get her way. Serena poses as Samantha again in the episode "Darrin Goes Ape."[27] Darrin has just rejected a gift from Serena, so Serena (as Samantha) says to him, "Sweetheart? You know, Serena really meant to be nice when she gave you that gift. People give the only way they know how, and Serena . . ." Darrin cuts her off, reminding her that she knows how he feels about that stuff. Serena (as Samantha) replies, "But Serena's really so sweet, and she means well." Darrin says, "she isn't just stubborn but rotten," and Serena gets mad and reveals herself. Darrin responds, "Serena, that's unfair; that's entrapment," and Serena informs him, "Ding-dong, you have all the gentility, graciousness, and gratitude of a gorilla, which is what you are about to become." Serena turns Darrin into an ape. In "Mrs. Stephens, Where Are You," Serena turns Phyllis Stephens into a cat when she begins to criticize Samantha and her family. When Samantha asks why, Serena answers, "Because she had her catty claws into all of us, including dear Uncle Arthur, who she practically accused of being the toss pot. You should hear what she said about you." Finally, when Serena isn't able to control her situation by turning people into animals, she makes unfair threats to get her way. In "Marriage, Witch's Style," Serena wants Samantha to go with her as she participates in a mortal dating service. Samantha doesn't want to be involved, so Serena says, "If you don't come with me, I'm going to tell Dumbo [Darrin] all about you and Sir Walter Raleigh." Surprised, Samantha replies, "But I've never even met Sir Walter Raleigh." Serena answers, "I know that—and you know that—but will he believe it?" Samantha says, "That's liar's blackmail."

Serena's loose inhibitions also function to align her with sixties counterculture, a culture that *Bewitched* often refers to as "hippie culture."[28] Thus, Serena's outfits and behaviors are often portrayed as hippie attire and hippie activities. To illustrate this point, several episodes align hippie culture with bad behavior. For example, in the episode "Hippie, Hippie Hooray," Darrin and Samantha are watching the news on television; the newscaster says, "We switch our scene to the county jail, where our elite of the hippie society is now in residence. Hippies and the police have had an active relationship in the past but nothing quite as active as today when the high priestess [Serena] of the movement did a vanishing act from the jail cell." In various ways, Serena is depicted as a hippie, and hippie culture is portrayed and accepted as countercultural. In "Cousin Serena Strikes Again, Part 1," Samantha and Darrin are asleep, when Serena rides into their living room on a motorcycle, suggesting that she is a member of a motorcycle gang. This representation would have made instant associations between Serena and the counterculture in the 1960s, as O'Neill indicates, public events of the decade would often be disrupted by motorcycle groups[29]—an interference that often made the news. This will be discussed later in the chapter. Returning to the episode, Darrin asks her what she is doing in the middle of the night, and Serena says, "I just came by to ask you to take a ride; Isn't it [the bike] the end?" Samantha angrily replies, "No, but you are. Do you realize it is three in the morning?" The episode "Mrs. Stephens, Where Are You" presents a similar treatment of Serena's wild behavior. Samantha leaves Serena in the house (to stay with Tabitha, who is sleeping) so that she can go look for Phyllis Stephens (Sam's mother-in-law), whom Serena has turned into a cat, and when Samantha returns home, she finds Serena in the living room doing a Go-Go dance wildly to loud rock and roll music, under the flairs of bright disco lights. Samantha asks her, "Serena, what are you trying to do? Deafen the whole neighborhood." Defiantly, Serena continues dancing and answers, "I haven't heard anyone complaining." Samantha says, "How could you hear anything over that music?" Again, Serena is depicted as a hippie who dances, listens to loud rock and roll music, and loves the disco—even while she is babysitting a sleeping child. The episode "Darrin on a Pedestal" has Samantha and Darrin traveling to Boston to support Endora, who is giving a speech. Serena shows up in their hotel room unannounced, and she is flying a small helicopter that is painted in wild and crazy colors and has Serena's name displayed boldly on the side. All of these examples firmly align Serena's character with qualities of sexual excess, an intense lack of self-control, and sixties counterculture.

CAREER INTERESTS

Bewitched engages with and responds to *The Feminine Mystique* through evil-twin depictions of career interests, as well. Samantha is a happy housewife most of the time, and her dialogue frequently reflects her satisfaction in this role of service, as she often says, "I love being a housewife." Serena, however, frequently pursues various forms of career interests, typically those involving performance, by which she attempts to dominate the public sphere, just as her opposite is content to serve in the private sphere.

Serena has several career interests. In the episode "Double, Double, Toil and Trouble,"[30] Endora uses dialogue to align Serena's character with evil. She says, "I've just had a perfectly marvelous, *evil* idea," as she summons Serena to appear before her. In other words, Serena *is* her "evil idea." She wants Serena to pose as Samantha, who is working all day at the church bazaar, thus neglecting her duties as queen of the Witches Council. Serena agrees and says, "I'll bet it will be more fun than the time I joined the Navy"—a statement that is a not-so-veiled comment about transgressing gender boundaries. When Endora claims that "this is business," Serena responds, "Yes, but I always manage to combine business with pleasure." The dialogue not only reveals Serena's career in the Navy, but her general interest in business/pleasure, as well—something typically reserved for male characters. Considering the idiom "never mix business with pleasure" is generally regarded as good advice for any responsible professional, the show uses Serena's desire to mix business and pleasure and disobey the "rules" of professionalism, as a way of rendering her individual career activities as selfish, irresponsible, and naughty.

Serena's involvement in competitions, performances of all kinds, and business ventures indicates her multitude of talent-based career interests. In "Samantha's Power Failure,"[31] for example, Serena shows up at the Stephens' house as a platinum-belt, karate master and claims to be on her way to India for the world rope-climbing championship. Later in the episode, Serena has her powers removed by the Witches Council for remaining loyal to Samantha, who is in "hot water" with them at the moment. Serena decides to get a job, and she begins working at an ice cream store. The manager shows her how to take a frozen banana and dip it in chocolate; Serena responds, "Oh, that should be easy. I'm a dipper from way back," indicating her experience as a pick-pocket. Her Uncle Arthur has started the job with her, and he responds, "Yeah, she used to be known as the big dipper." In "Serena Stops the Show," Serena has been elected as the "entertainment chairman for the Cosmos Cotillion." She wants to employ the popular band Boyce and Hart to perform in the Cotillion, and she tries to lure them by performing the original song she wrote for them. Later, when Serena shows them the sheet music for the song, they ask, "What are all these little black marks?" She responds, "Don't you two read music?" They do not, yet she understands music well enough to compose and perform. At the end of the episode, Samantha appears and tells Serena to send those "howling hippies back to earth"—again establishing Serena's behavior as countercultural in nature. In the episode "Darrin on a Pedestal," Serena shows up in the helicopter of many colors and claims she has been participating in the world kite-flying championship. She says, "I'm sorry I was late, but I got involved in India's kite-flying championship and guess what? I was disqualified on a mere technicality. Instead of flying it, I toted it." Thus, she is not just interested in participating in competitions, she has a penchant for breaking the rules. Similarly, in "Chance on Love," Serena tries to convince Samantha to quit her housework and attend a different kind of competition, saying, "Instead, why don't you break out and join me and the maharaja Manipur. He's throwing an elephant race." Finally, in "Serena's Youth Pill," Samantha summons Serena, asking her to fill in for her at the charity luncheon. Frustrated, Serena asks, "Charity luncheon? Do you realize that the French fleet at Saint-Tropez was about to crown me Miss Naval?" Samantha responds, saying, "Well, I'm sorry, Serena, but your trophy room is overflowing as it is," indicating how often Serena pursues her own interests in these ways. Later, Serena develops and administers to Larry a pill she calls "Vitamin V" for "Va-va-voom." She says it will put the color back in his hair and the bloom of youth back in his cheeks. He agrees to take the pill, and Serena asks him to stick around because "that pill's a fast worker, and so am I."

Serena's career interests are underscored by the fact that Samantha never desires to perform, to write music for famous bands, to learn karate, or to compete in kite-flying or other competitions. Other than housewifery, Samantha pursues activities such as volunteering in the church bazaar and selling raffle tickets for Darrin's company. Even her extracurricular activities are service-oriented, while Serena's pursuits involve working toward personal goals and interests.[32] As by-products of independence, the Friedan split places these qualities on the evil side because the personal goals and interests are regarded as taking time and effort away from the home and marriage— woman's only acceptable priorities.

POLITICAL INTERESTS

Although the episodes reflecting the evil-twin interests in political issues are few in number, one example is worth mentioning. In the episode "Hippie, Hippie, Hooray," Serena is arrested because she has been leading a hippie "love-in," which develops into a riot after a motorcycle gang invades. A picture of her being arrested for involvement in this event makes the front page of the newspaper—another instance of the evil twin making a public declaration and putting herself on display in a public venue far from the realm of the domestic sphere. This episode aligns Serena with the 1960s counterculture explicitly, as the show aired on February 1st, 1968, during a time when the counterculture was often defined as anti-establishment groups who engaged in peace movements, teach-ins, and hippie lifestyles. Just under three years prior to the airing of the episode, in March of 1965, the first teach-in—the peace movement's initial response to the Vietnam War—was held at the University of Michigan; this and subsequent teach-ins provided opportunities for individuals to engage in anti-war rhetoric. In many cases, as O'Neill identifies, these events would be disrupted by motorcycle groups and end in riots: "During the October 1965 peace demonstrations, it [the Vietnam Day Committee] marched on Oakland and was attacked by both the police and motorcycle hoodlums. When the VDC planned another march for November 20, the Hell's Angels promised to destroy it entirely."[33] The episode reflects this history precisely and is significant for multiple reasons. First, through political interest, the series identifies Serena as part of the counterculture, as part of the "them" segment in an "us vs. them" society. It also shows that Serena's interests in social and political matters are direct threats to a woman's function within the home, as Serena's protest, while peaceful, results in prison time. Samantha makes this point even more explicit when, rather than expressing concern for her cousin's safety in prison, her only concern is how Serena's public actions will upset Darrin, who is, as she claims, "traditional." In this way, Serena's desire to be politically active is depicted as silly, irresponsible, a threat to the home, and ultimately, evil.

INTELLECTUAL PROWESS

I have titled this category as such in an effort to create a section that accommodates many of Friedan's words on the matter. In describing traits that belong to the evil side of the split—traits viewed by popular culture as impediments to a woman realizing her full potential—she says, "the only problems now are those that might disturb her adjustment as a housewife. So career is a problem, education is a problem, political interest, even the very admission of women's intelligence and individuality is a problem."[34] In this category of "Intellectual Prowess," I include travel, in addition to more formal types of education and signs of intelligence, in general. In other words, I am claiming that the alter egos, in being depicted as both intelligent and manipulative, are confirming Friedan's assessment that American popular culture regards intelligence and education in women as indicators of the evil of independence, as traits belonging to the evil side of Friedan's split.

In *Bewitched*, Serena has been on a safari in Kenya in the episode "Marriage, Witches' Style," and when she babysits Samantha's children in the episode "Samantha and the Troll,"[35] she counts in French for a game of "hide and seek" and plays the piano like a virtuoso for a game of "ring-around-the-rosy." Serena's experiences and abilities imply not only that she has been educated in foreign travel, languages, and music, but also that she has mastered these areas. Even though Serena's education is typically presented in snippets such as this, one episode reveals her formal education directly. In "Serena's Richcraft,"[36] Serena has been stripped of her powers, but she attempts to seduce Darrin's wealthy client, Harrison Woolcut, anyway. He owns many hotels, and she claims to have stayed in the New York, Tokyo, Istanbul, and San Francisco locations, reflecting again her diverse travels. Consequently, Woolcut asks Serena to go boating with him on his yacht. When she gets on board, she immediately recognizes the artists of his paintings—Picasso, Matisse, and Van Gogh—and identifies the works as copies. Harrison asks her how she knows, and she says, "Vincent never caressed a canvas; he attacked it" and claims to have done her "thesis on Van Gogh." Later in the episode, Harrison asks, "Where did you get your education?" Serena impulsively responds, "Witches U," but then catches her mistake and says that's her name for Vassar, where they "had a real witch for a Dean." Not only is Serena portrayed as being formally educated, her education operates as a signifier of evil, since she uses it explicitly to manipulate and seduce Woolcut. Serena exhibits a similar high-culture savvy in "Marriage, Witch's Style." She uses a mortal dating service to find a date, and on the date, she is asked about her favorite wine. She says it is "Chateau La Vie Rothchild 1923." When she calls to tell Samantha about him, Samantha asks if he is intelligent. Serena admits that this is one of her favorite things about him, claiming, "Intelligent? He's read books that haven't even been written yet!" In the same episode, Serena tells Samantha, "Tomorrow, I'm off to Balmoral with [Queen] Elizabeth and Philip, and on the weekend, I'm expected in Athens for a yacht christening." Wine, books, and travel are all used as indications of Serena's intelligence. In "Samantha's Psychic Slip,"[37] Serena recognizes that Samantha needs to see a doctor for a checkup, so she calls on Dr. Bombay (Bernard Fox). Once Samantha is better, Serena says, "I think I'll cut out. I have a date to play chess." Samantha asks, "Since when have you taken up chess," and Serena answers, "Since I found a set with real kings." All of these episodes serve as examples of Serena's multitude of intellectual, high-culture experiences.

ASSERTIVENESS

The final category of assertiveness is reflected in Serena throughout the series. When she wants something, she immediately pursues it, and she resists being told what to do in almost any capacity. In the following examples, Serena asserts herself and cautions males against trying to dominate her; that said, the episodes portray Serena's intentions as being manipulative, rather than strong. In the episode "Hippie, Hippie, Hooray," Serena is babysitting Tabitha, and she teaches Tabitha a rock-n-roll version of the song "Rock-a-bye Baby." Darrin forbids this, and Serena responds to him, "When you use words like 'forbid' with me . . . smile." Through this statement, Serena asserts her dislike for Darrin's dominance and condescension, implying that, unless he is kidding, she will not allow him to command her in the same way he commands Samantha. Similarly, in the episode "A Chance on Love,"[38] Serena is posing as Samantha to sell raffle tickets, when the businessman George Tisdale begins to flirt with her, saying, "Might I say, you are the wildest game I've ever hunted." Serena responds, "Careful. Maybe you're the chicken and I'm the hawk." Finally, the strongest example of Serena asserting herself is in the episode "Double, Double Toil and Trouble." Samantha is serving as queen of the Witches Council, but Darrin will not allow the ceremony to take her away from her duties at home. When she attempts to hold a meeting in the living room, Darrin asks her to get rid of everyone. Endora and Serena develop a plan to allow Samantha to fulfill her witch duties without upsetting Darrin. Endora says, "I've just had a perfectly marvelous evil idea." She summons Serena, who appears with her same short dark hair, wearing a "far-out" bright pink and green mini dress, bright pink heels, and matching tights. Serena asks Endora, "Is cousin Samantha gone? Oh, this is going to be a ball." Endora replies, "Serena, we are not here to have fun. You are here to do a job, now remember that." Serena changes her outfit and hair to match Samantha, which involves changing to blonde hair, white shoes, a soft pink knee-length dress, and a white purse—a look that Serena visibly doesn't like. Serena (as Samantha) walks through the front door, and Darrin is surprised to see her. He sits down on couch and pats the cushion next to him, saying, "Come here and give us a kiss." Serena responds, "If you want a kiss, come and get it." Darrin says, "okay" and walks over to her, but when he goes in for a kiss, she magically moves herself to the stairs. He tries the kiss again on the stairs, but she magically moves herself to the floor. Frustrated, Darrin asks, "Hey, what's the big idea?" Serena moves a chair in front of her so that Darrin can't get to her. He asks, "Have you flipped? What's gotten into you?" Serena replies, "Nothing, I just didn't feel like being pawed." Darrin assumes that she is still sore about the argument they had the night before, and he reminds her that he apologized. The doorbell rings, and when Darrin goes to answer it, Serena moves a rug in front of him, so that he trips and falls to the ground. All of these examples reflect Leibman's claim that characters "who adopt those [traits] belonging to the opposite sex, are deemed dysfunctional (if they are men) or evil (if they are women)."[39] Serena challenges patriarchal hegemony by asserting her position and unwillingness to be dominated.

To be fair, there are moments in the series where Samantha chides Darrin for his need to dominate, but she never does so as explicitly as Serena or Endora. The episode "It's So Nice to Have a Spouse Around the House"[40] provides a typical example of how Samantha engages in dialogue about this subject. Samantha is in the kitchen cooking, when her apron disappears. Samantha says, "Mother," and Endora appears and notifies her that she needs to appear before the Witches Council. However, Darrin forbids it, saying to Samantha, "Let's get some things straight. First, you're a wife. Then, you're a witch. And a wife's place is with her husband." Samantha replies in a way that is atypically sarcastic for her, saying, "Oh, good. I guess that means you want me to play golf with you this afternoon." Darrin yells back, "You know what I mean!" Similarly, in "Tabitha's Very Own Samantha," Samantha tells Darrin how much Tabitha helped her that day and that she is going to take her to the play park the next day. Darrin asks, "You don't think you're overcompensating?" Samantha answers, "Not at all. Tabitha needs to learn that the women around here have equal rights, no matter how handsome the men are." Significantly, these episodes are two of the 13.3 percent of the series written by women. Barbara Avedon wrote the first example— when Samantha's response to Darrin voices what viewers suspect to be her *actual* inner feelings each time Darrin reminds her of her "wifely duties"—and Shirley Gordon wrote the latter example—when Samantha reminds Darrin of the equal rights of women. It is telling that responses such as these often occur when the scripts involve the input of women, but I will save the analysis of how female-written episodes differ from male-written ones for the fifth chapter. The episode "The Corsican Cousins" provides a similar, but perhaps less powerful, example. Darrin has decided that he and Samantha should join the local country club. The application process requires that he play a round of golf with the men, so that they can get to know him, and Samantha has to entertain the women at her home, so that they can assess her abilities and situation. Upon hearing this, Samantha says to Darrin, "I have an idea. How about I play golf and you entertain the ladies?" Even though this episode was written by Ed Jurist, it serves to use Samantha's dialogue to acknowledge and underscore the inequities of male and female roles regarding social obligations. Since the male role is to dominate the public sphere, Darrin is judged by the other men in that sphere—a sphere that requires no preparation or work, only play. Meanwhile, the woman is allowed to dominate only the private sphere, which is why the other women must judge Samantha in that realm. Her task involves cleaning, cooking, serving, entertaining, and being constantly aware of the needs of others in her home throughout the extent of their visit—an experience that would never be considered "play time." The two "interviews" are completely unmatched, and Samantha's dialogue serves to highlight that inequity. Ed Jurist seems to have been a male writer who was uniquely aware of these husband/wife dynamics. In another of his episodes, "The Return of Darrin the Bold,"[41] Darrin wakes up from a nap on the couch, saying to Samantha, "That's alright. I don't want to sleep the whole day. There are things I want to do around the house, like fix those tiles in the kitchen." Samantha tells him, "I already fixed the tiles . . . I got tired of tripping over them." Darrin responds, "Sweetheart, you don't understand. You aren't supposed to fix things like that. That's man's work." Samantha asks, "Even a man who has been putting it off for months?" Jokingly, Darrin replies, "You don't understand. You see, putting it off is also man's work." Jurist clearly had a distinctive voice that comedically tapped into dominant gender issues of the decade.

CONCLUSIONS

Bewitched is the strongest example of television reflecting and producing Friedan's split included in this study. It is the highest rated and longest-running series analyzed herein, and it includes more evil-twin episodes and female television writers than any other show. Whereas this chapter identifies the specific ways in which the character Serena appears to have been created to align with the characteristics of the evil side of Friedan's split and Samantha with the good side, the one thing all of Serena's examples have in common is her perpetual desire to dominate in the public sphere—a desire that would have still deemed her countercultural by 1960s societal standards—instead of being content in the private sphere. Serena rarely plays by the rules that have been established for her, especially throughout the 1950s. As I've mentioned, to underscore her countercultural function, instead of continuing to credit Montgomery as Serena's actress, the show began claiming Serena was played by "Pandora Spocks," a name that obviously indicates Serena's function as a Pandora's box. This detail is revealing. The precise definition of a Pandora's box is that it involves a process that generates complications because of an *unwise interference* in something. Serena's desire to function in the public sphere provides an unwise interference in the prescribed social order—a system that insists women must find satisfaction within the private sphere in order to allow the men to succeed in the public sphere. Serena transgresses gender boundaries, and her transgressions always result in complications.

Furthermore, she is rarely accepted by those around her. In fact, the writers take Serena even a bit further than just wanting to function in the public sphere through karate, kite-flying, rope-climbing championships, yacht christenings, meetings with the Queen of England, elephant races, naval assignments, songwriting, performances, and safaris. Serena actually rejects the private sphere. This is evidenced in "Cousin Serena Strikes Again, Part 2," when Samantha indicates that, one day, Serena will want Samantha to babysit her own children, and Serena responds, "I sincerely hope not." Similarly, in the first "Serena" episode, "And Then There Were Three," Serena believes a real centaur is an appropriate gift for a newborn baby, only to be corrected by new-mom Samantha; when Samantha needs her help in "It's So Nice to Have a Spouse Around the House," she begs Serena to "just be a housewife for a few hours"—a request that makes Serena cringe. She also cringes when Samantha reminds her that mortal men "absolutely love helpless women," in the episode "Marriage, Witches Style"—an episode that, written by a male writer, indicates the American male's knowledge of the American woman's awareness of and willingness to accommodate his need to dominate. In "Serena's Richcraft," Serena tries to use a basic kitchen mixer; the results are disastrous, and the mixer flings food all over the room. Finally, in "Hippie, Hippie Hooray," again, Serena exemplifies her domestic ineptitude; when asked to put Tabitha to sleep, Serena sings and plays lullabies to rock and roll music instead of soothing music. Thus, Serena's character often serves to reject domesticity completely.

Serena's attire contributes greatly to these interpretations. She is often dressed in clothing that is reminiscent of hunted, thus dominated, animals. Her outfits underscore her conversation with "George" in the episode "Chance on Love." While they are on a date, George starts talking about hunting. Serena replies, "Don't tell me you're a hunter too," and George says, "You're the wildest thing I've ever hunted." Serena quickly cautions him, advising, "Be careful; you may find that you're the chicken and I'm the hawk." Indeed, the series uses iconography and dialogue to identify Serena as the predator—not the prey. From her first episode to her last, Serena wears large feather boas and fur coats—all outfits that reflect the spoils of the hunt and label her as a hunter, as a dominator. In "Marriage, Witches Style," she is wearing a fur coat that is clearly the skin of a tiger, and she tells Samantha that she has been on a safari in Kenya and asks if she likes the coat. In "And Then There Were Three," Serena is first presented in a long, solid black fur coat, aligning her with both hunting and darkness. In "Generation Zap," Serena arrives with a larger-than-life boa made of what appears to be brown and white turkey feathers. In almost every depiction, Serena dons the rewards of her hunts, whether they be in fur or feather form. Her role as a predator is furthered again in the episode "Tabitha's Very Own Samantha," when Samantha attempts to quiet Darrin, who is being critical of Serena, by saying, "Shhh . . . She may still be hanging around." Darrin responds, "Sure, from a rafter in the attic," identifying Serena as a bat-like, thus vampire-like and blood-sucking, creature.

In addition to depicting Serena as a hunter, which transgresses gender roles already, all of her adventures involve the public sphere, in general; thus, her major flaw is not being too sexual or 'hippie'; it is her desire to maintain an involvement in the male public sphere that consistently gets her into trouble. Last, I use the episode "Darrin, the Ape" to transition from one enormously popular sitcom, *Bewitched*, to another, *I Dream of Jeannie*. In this episode, Serena has turned Darrin into an ape, and when the police arrive at the house, Serena appears next to them in a safari outfit. The police officer asks, "where did you come from?" Serena responds, "Originally, Babylon." Thus, Samantha, Serena, Jeannie, and Sister Jeannie all originated in the same location. Babylon is the most famous city of ancient Mesopotamia, and its ruins lie near modern-day Baghdad. In the aforementioned episode, Serena indicates that she is originally from Babylon, and in the *I Dream of Jeannie* episode, "Genie, Genie, Who's Got the Genie?, Part 3," Sister Jeannie indicates she is from Baghdad. She intentionally mixes up Tony's next assignment, so that instead of going to his intended location near the equator, sister Jeannie changes things and says, "I have just arranged for master to be assigned to the Middle East. Once I get him on my home turf in Baghdad, he's going to have a hard time helping himself." Thus, the witches and genies from both series all come from the same foreign location—modern day Iraq.[42] This detail taps into issues of Orientalism—a term coined by Edward Said that connects feminism to issues of gender construction, social construction, colonialism, and otherness:

> We can now see that Orientalism is a praxis of the same sort, albeit in different territories, as male gender dominance, or patriarchy, in metropolitan societies: the Orient was routinely described as feminine, its riches as fertile, its main symbols the sensual woman, the harem and the despotic—but curiously attractive—ruler. Moreover, Orientals, like Victorian housewives, were confined to silence and to unlimited enriching production.[43]

As Katharine Bullock argues of Jeannie in *I Dream of Jeannie*, Orientalism is "at the core"[44] of the show and serves to "other" her and her culture. American culture accepts her, though, because she is sensual *and* fertile, desiring first and foremost to serve her "master" and maintain the "Victorian housewife silence" of her desires—which endears her to mid-century American audiences. However, Sister Jeannie is the opposite—she does not desire to produce or serve; she lives a life of unabashed excess; and she usually reverts to typical male despotic behaviors of power and control. I believe a similar treatment is used with Serena in *Bewitched*. Serena and Sister Jeannie are often so similar that one could argue that Sister Jeannie's character was modeled after Serena.[45] They both refer to their twins as abbreviated names, "Cuz" or "Sis," and they use the word "Poopsie" often when talking to men—a name that is typically used as a term of endearment for a small child. When the evil twins call men "Poopsie," they are establishing a power dynamic that is inconsistent with the social order, thus "othering" themselves even further. Ultimately, these similarities further indicate a strong through-line that serves to tether all three of these shows to each other: Sheldon created and wrote *The Patty Duke Show*; Asher directed most of the episodes of the first season of that show; Asher moved on to direct *Bewitched*, and on the heels of its success, Sheldon created and wrote another American television hit featuring twins: *I Dream of Jeannie*.

NOTES

1. *I Married a Witch*, written by Robert Pirosh and Marc Connelly (screenplay), directed by René Clair, starring Veronica Lake, 1942.

2. *Bell, Book, and Candle*, written by Daniel Taradash (screenplay) and John Van Druten (play), directed by Richard Quine, December 1958.

3. The now famous *Bewitched* intro tune was composed by Jack Keller. It originally had lyrics by Howard Greenfield, but the lyrics were never used.

4. This ever-changing beauty mark takes the form of a heart, a treble cleft, a question mark, an exclamation point, a peace sign, and an anchor, to name a few examples.

5. One example of Montgomery's influence involves the character of her daughter, Tabitha. Apparently, producers originally desired that her name be spelled "Tabatha," but Montgomery insisted and eventually had the name spelling changed to Tabitha.

6. This argument is put forward by Nine C. Leibman in *Living Room Lectures*.

7. Susan Douglas makes this claim in *Where the Girls Are*.

8. Leibman, *Living Room Lectures*, 195.

9. Hall, *Representation*, 24.

10. *Bewitched*, season 2, episode 18, "And Then There Were Three," written by Bernard Slade, directed by William Asher, January 1966.

11. *Bewitched*, season 5, episode 16, "Cousin Serena Strikes Again, Part 2," written by Ed Jurist, directed by Richard Michaels, January 1969.

12. *Bewitched*, season 5, episode 21, "Marriage, Witches' Style," written by Michael Morris, directed by William Asher, February 1969.

13. Humphreys, "Supernatural Housework," 109.

14. *Bewitched*, season 7, episode 21, "Mixed Doubles," written by Richard Baer, directed by William Asher, March 1971.

15. *Bewitched*, season 2, episode 21, "Fastest Gun on Madison Avenue," written by Lee Erwin, directed by William Asher, February 1966.

16. *Bewitched*, season 6, episode 26, "Chance on Love," written by John L. Greene, directed by Richard Michaels, March 1970.

17. *Bewitched*, season 7, episode 11, "The Corsican Cousins," written by Ed Jurist, directed by Richard Michaels, December 1970.

18. *Bewitched*, season 5, episode 20, "Mrs. Stephens, Where Are You," written by Peggy Chantler Dick and Douglas Dick, directed by Richard Michaels, February 1969.

19. *Bewitched*, season 7, episode 5, "Darrin on a Pedestal," written by Bernie Kahn, directed by William Asher, October 1970.

20. The episodes "Tony's Wife" (Season Three; Writ. Christopher Golato) from *Jeannie* and "Serena's Richcraft" (Season Eight; Writ. Michael Morris) from *Bewitched* provide additional examples for this section. Regarding "independence" specifically, episodes "My Sister the Homewrecker" (Season Five; Writ. James Henerson) from *Jeannie*, "Double, Double, Toil and Trouble," and especially, "Marriage, Witches' Style," (Season Five; Writ. Michael Morris) from *Bewitched* provide examples.

21. *Bewitched*, season 5, episode 2, "Samantha Goes South for a Spell," written by Ed Jurist, directed by William Asher, October 1968.

22. *Bewitched*, season 7, episode 4, "Samantha's Hot Bedwarmer," written by Ed Jurist, directed by William Asher, October 1970.

23. *Bewitched*, season 6, episode 22, "Serena Stops the Show," written by Richard Baer, directed by Richard Michaels, February 1970.

24. *Bewitched*, season 8, episode 19, "Serena's Youth Pill," written by Michael Morris, directed by E.W. Swackhamer, February 1972.

25. *Bewitched*, season 5, episode 16, "Cousin Serena Strikes Again, Part 2," written by Ed Jurist, directed by Richard Michaels, January 1969.

26. *Bewitched*, season 6, episode 26, "Chance on Love," written by John L. Greene, directed by Richard Michaels, March 1970.

27. *Bewitched*, season 7, episode 22, "Darrin Goes Ape," written by Leo and Pauline Townsend, directed by Richard Michaels, March 1971.

28. One example is in the episode "George Washington Zapped Here, Part 1" (written by Michael Morris and directed by Richard Michaels). Esmeralda has zapped George Washington from the past into the present. When Washington begins walking around town, a policeman stops him and threatens to arrest him, thinking he is either drunk or crazy. The policeman indicates that he can handle whatever craziness Washington gives him because the policeman has "dealt with all kinds of hippies." Episodes such as this align hippies with "crazy," countercultural behavior.

29. O'Neill, *Coming Apart*, 144.

30. *Bewitched*, season 4, episode 4, "Double, Double, Toil and Trouble," written by Ed Jurist, directed by William Asher, September 1967.

31. *Bewitched*, season 5, episode 25, "Samantha's Power Failure," written by Lila Garrett and Bernie Kahn, directed by William Asher, March 1969.

32. The *Bewitched* episode "Hippie, Hippie, Hooray," season four, written by Michael Morris, provides an additional example for this section.

33. O'Neill, *Coming Apart*, 144.

34. Friedan, *The Feminine Mystique*, 61.

35. *Bewitched*, season 7, episode 19, "Samantha and the Troll," written by Lila Garrett and Joel Rapp, directed by William Asher, February 1971.

36. *Bewitched*, season 8, episode 17, "Serena's Richcraft," written by Michael Morris, directed by William Asher, January 1972.

37. *Bewitched*, season 7, episode 25, "Samantha's Psychic Slip," written by John L. Greene, directed by William Asher, April 1971.

38. *Bewitched*, season 6, episode 26, "Chance on Love," written by John L. Greene, directed by Richard Michaels, March 1970.

39. Leibman, *Living Room Lectures*, 174.

40. *Bewitched*, season 5, episode 5, "It's So Nice to Have a Spouse Around the House," written by Barbara Avedon, directed by William Asher, October 1968.

41. *Bewitched*, season 7, episode 17, "The Return of Darrin the Bold," written by Ed Jurist, directed by Richard Michaels, February 1971.

42. In the *I Dream of Jeannie* episode "G.I. Jeannie," Jeannie identifies Pompeii as her place of birth, but more often, it is indicated as Baghdad.

43. Edward Said, "Orientalism Reconsidered," *Cultural Critique* (fall 1985), 103.

44. Katharine Bullock, "Orientalism on Television: A Case Study of *I Dream of Jeannie*," in *ReOrient*, 10/2018, Volume 4, Issue 1, 4.

45. The first Serena episode of *Bewitched* aired in January of 1966, and the first Sister Jeannie episode aired in September of 1967, so a year and a half separate the two.

3

I Dream of Jeannie

Following a successful first season of *Bewitched* and while still writing for *The Patty Duke Show*, Sheldon was asked to create another show, one that could resemble *Bewitched*, featuring twins with supernatural abilities: *I Dream of Jeannie*. After refusing to marry a djinn, Jeannie (Barbara Eden) is exiled to a bottle for 2000 years. Astronaut Tony Nelson (Larry Hagman) finds the bottle on an island during a mission and frees Jeannie, who says he is her new master. Even though Tony tells her in this first episode that she may be free, she claims that she does not want to be free but would rather serve him—a not-so-veiled comment on gender issues of the era. In addition to Jeannie, Eden, like Patty Duke in *The Patty Duke Show*, portrays two additional characters—her evil sister, Jeannie, and their mother. While *I Dream of Jeannie* didn't quite attain the popularity of *Bewitched*, it did well enough for Nielsen ratings to place it in the top 30 for multiple seasons. It has enjoyed a great deal of popularity in syndication, as well. The show first aired in September of 1965 and ran until May of 1970, producing 139 episodes over five seasons.

In a 2006 article in *Variety* titled "The gentleman preferred a blonde," Jenny Peters interviewed Eden about Sheldon and his casting choices. Eden remembers that the production team had been "testing all these Middle-Eastern, tall and gorgeous women [for the role of Jeannie]—Miss Morocco, Miss Lebanon, Miss Italy—all brunettes and all very tall."[1] Eden recalls wondering why she, being "blonde and short," was being called in to read for the role. In her autobiography, *Jeannie, Out of the Bottle*, Eden discussed the casting further:

> Sure, I'd read about *I Dream of Jeannie* in the trade press, that it was a fantasy about a female genie, but there was nothing in the article about any bottle yet, or what kind of an actress the show's creator, writer, and producer, Sidney Sheldon, was planning to cast as his Jeannie. The word, though, through the grapevine, was that he and the show's

Figure 3.1. Barbara Eden as Jeannie wears what eventually becomes Sister Jeannie's green harem outfit, in *I Dream of Jeannie*, AF Archive / Alamy Stock Photo

producers were holding clandestine meetings with Miss Greece, Miss Israel, and other sultry five-foot-nine beauty queens with a view to auditioning them for the part. I never dreamed that Sidney would consider me for the role of Jeannie. But then I didn't know that he'd seen *Brass Bottle*, or that we had a number of mutual friends who were comedy writers and seemed to like and admire my work.[2]

Brass Bottle is a 1964 film that features a male genie who wants to help his master but ultimately causes more trouble than good. Eden had a supporting role in the film, but it was enough to get her noticed by Sheldon.

Even without *Brass Bottle*, though, Eden credits Sheldon for being able to think outside of the box, when it comes to casting. Sheldon's choice in Eden is important because throughout the series, almost every single woman who serves as a threat to Jeannie's relationship with Tony is depicted with dark hair. In the pilot episode, Tony is engaged to be married to a dark-haired Melissa Stone (Karen Sharpe). Jeannie refers to her as a "black-haired witch" and a "black-haired demon." Her dialogue always associates her dark hair with hell and thus, evil. And Stone is actually a very sexual character, as she even tries to move up the wedding date so that she and Tony can get to the more physical activities that are reserved for husbands and wives. Similarly, in "G.I. Jeannie,"[3] Tony is assigned a new secretary, Corporal Burns, who is a dark-headed bombshell. She begins flirting with Tony on the first day of the job, and Jeannie looks for ways to have her replaced.

All of these characters lead up to Sister Jeannie having dark hair and embodying evil, but before Sister could make her first appearance, the show needed to establish firmly Jeannie's wholesomeness, so as to place her unequivocally on the good side of the split and in opposition to sister's evil. Considering Eden was naturally a sexually appealing person, this proved to be tricky when it came to Jeannie's sexuality. Eden recalls the challenges:

> *I Dream of Jeannie* is actually one of the most daring shows on TV. It is the only show, for example, in which an attractive unmarried girl has the free run of a bachelor's apartment. And as far as NBC was concerned, the matter of Jeannie and morality had to be taken extremely seriously in the show—as seriously as if she were a real-life woman and the story we were telling was fact, not a figment of Sidney's deliciously overwrought imagination . . . This is what NBC decreed so as to preserve the moral tone of *I Dream of Jeannie*: (1) It was imperative that my harem trousers be lined with silk so my legs didn't show through the transparent fabric. (2) Jeannie's smoke was banned from disappearing under Captain Nelson's bedroom door. (3) Openmouthed kissing between Tony and his fiancée, Melissa, was banned. (4) Nor was Jeannie permitted to be provocative or flirtatious . . . I never considered Jeannie to be provocative or flirtatious, by the way, because I always thought of her as a tomboy, not a vamp.[4]

Eden also recalled that when she would have lines such as, "I am going to please thee very much," in an effort to avoid the sexual innuendo, the network would request she be more specific, by indicating how she would please (e.g., with jewels, money, etc.). Even with these accommodations, the sexual innuendos did not go unnoticed. For example, *Variety* reviewed the first episode, saying, "Miss Eden plays a genie who materializes out of an Egyptian jug to badger an astronaut, making his commanding officers believe he's off his rocker, driving his fiancée up the wall, and teasing viewers with dirty minds with innuendo."[5] Critics weren't necessarily impressed, and the network had low expectations for the show in general, which is evidenced by the fact that they insisted on shooting the first season in black and white, while most shows were being shot in color at the time, even with color costing about $400 more per episode. The network didn't want to make that kind of investment on a show they weren't sure would succeed. Sheldon even offered to put up his own money to have it shot in color, but he ultimately decided against it. The expectations of the network and the assessments of the television critics didn't matter, though, because audiences loved the show, which is why it lasted longer than other series that received great reviews and lots of network funding.

Even beyond the casting elements and the network demands, the episodes preceding sister-Jeannie episodes worked to establish Jeannie as good, servile, caring, and domestic—a master of the private sphere—and as possessing no qualities that allow her to function successfully in the male-dominated public sphere. Throughout these episodes, Tony tells Jeannie to "be a good girl" and "stay home," and Jeannie is always asking Tony how she may serve him, even telling him in the episode "Jeannie and the Marriage Caper"[6] that "cooking is woman's work," so she wants to do the cooking and cleaning. Simultaneously, she is depicted as antithetical to the public sphere, unable to function in public without causing trouble. In the episode "G.I. Jeannie" again, Jeannie decides she wants to join the Women's Air Force, but Tony tells her she can't type or even take dictation. Determined, she applies and is given five aptitude tests—the same tests they give all of the recruits to determine their interests and abilities. Jeannie is told that all five tests indicate that she is not good at anything. Still, they assign her to a position as a nurse's aide, but she breaks a doctor's leg on the first day. Then, she is assigned to drive the jeep, but she immediately crashes it into a wall. She fails at every attempt to perform a function outside of the home. In the episode "The Americanization of Jeannie"—an episode that Sarah Kornfield astutely identifies as "a feminist doppelgänger that depicts feminism as illogical, apolitical, and ultimately comedic, thereby functioning to contain the cultural representations of feminism in the public forum"[7]—Jeannie decides she wants to become a "modern American woman." In a magazine spread titled "The Emancipation of Modern Woman," Jeannie reads that, to make men want her, she must follow certain steps toward becoming independent and self-reliant. She does so, as only she knows how. When Tony arrives home from work that day, he finds that the house is a mess and that Jeannie is wearing a robe, slippers, and curlers in her hair, eating chocolate. Tony asks if she forgot to do the housework, and Jeannie says, "I didn't forget. I decided to let you do it." Then she reads the magazine aloud and uses Friedan's term "drudge," just as *Bewitched* does; Jeannie reads, "How not to be a drudge. Share the work with him." Then, her new wardrobe of clothes, which includes a mink coat (note the connection to evil-twin affinities for furs and Jeannie's transformation to a feminist), arrives by delivery person at the front door—all of which she has purchased using Tony's credit card. At this point, Tony calls her magazine "subversive literature." They go out to dinner, and this is the first time Tony takes her out on deliberate public display. However, the "new" Jeannie won't let Tony order for her and begins drinking and shouting, and when she engages in conversation, she tells Tony about how she used to go wild-boar hunting with Marco Polo (again, note that writers are ascribing the evil-twin role as hunter/predator to Jeannie's character, as she attempts to become an "Emancipated Woman"/feminist). Then, when the restaurant's entertainment ends up being a dark-haired dancer who keeps flirting with Tony, Jeannie jumps onto the stage and embarrassingly attempts to "out-dance" her: all actions that force Tony to take her immediately back home, where he tells her that her behavior that night was "disgraceful," implying that "feminist behavior" is also disgraceful. Later, Jeannie gets a job selling appliances, but she causes a scene with customers and is fired on the first day. Jeannie simply cannot function in the public sphere. It is also worth noting that the show actually displays the "feminization" of Jeannie—Jeannie's foray into feminism—but titles the episode the "Americanization" of Jeannie—a choice that immediately connects Americanism with feminism. This will be explored in subsequent chapters. Similarly, in the episode "The Moving Finger,"[8] Jeannie auditions for a film by doing a screen test, but because of her supernatural qualities, she cannot be captured on film. The episode renders her literally invisible in her attempt to attain public attention. In all of these examples, Jeannie has not only attempted to dominate the public sphere, she has served to represent 1960s feminism. All of the traits she exhibits in these episodes—traits that always cause trouble—are later transferred to Sister Jeannie, once that character is developed. One could easily argue, then, that Sister Jeannie represents American television's opinion of sixties feminism.

The first episode featuring Jeannie's evil twin sister, also Jeannie, aired in the third season in September of 1967, about a year and a half after the first Serena episode of *Bewitched* and about four years after the first episode of *The Patty Duke Show*. Thus, in only four years, American television producers (mainly under the influence of Sheldon and Asher) created three popular series involving female twins, one good and one evil. It is understandable why the trend would continue, when the trope seemed to meet with such success each and every time. The first episode featuring Jeannie's sister Jeannie was "Jeannie or the Tiger?" written by James Henerson. The title alone places Jeannie and her sister in opposition—Jeannie, the servile domestic goddess or Sister Jeannie, the tiger/predator. A few years later, Henerson wrote the script for a film titled *The Feminist and the Fuzz* (1970), starring Barbara Eden as the "feminist" and produced by longtime *I Dream of Jeannie* director, Claudio Guzman. This film says a great deal about Henerson and the *Jeannie* production team being in conversation with feminism. In this film, Eden plays a pediatrician, Dr. Jane Bowers, and David Hartman plays the police officer, Jerry Frazer. Both characters are searching for an affordable apartment in San Francisco, even though it would seem they should be on two very different budgets (pediatrician and police officer), and they are simultaneously notified about the same apartment vacancy in two very different ways. Jerry arrives at the scene of an accident, where a self-described "hippie" admits he has been evicted from his apartment because the landlord doesn't like hippies, and Jane is given the tip about the apartment by a male colleague, who says he wants a dinner date in exchange for the information. Jane asks, "Don't you ever give up?" He responds, "A beautiful woman in the women's liberation movement is a challenge to me. Before you came along, I thought they were all army sergeants." This statement connects the film to chapter 4 and Emma's Army Sergeant depiction in *The Brady Bunch* episode "Sergeant Emma," which aired around the same time as *The Feminist and the Fuzz*. Jane rushes to see the apartment, and Jerry stops her for running a red light; after giving her a warning, he says, "Miss, you ought to be more careful. You're a beautiful girl. I can't think of a quicker way to lose your looks than getting smacked broadside because you ran a red light." The dialogue indicates that, as a film and television writer, Henerson was persistently in conversation with feminism, and this reality thus influences our interpretation of both Sister Jeannie's character and provides potential reasons she was created so oppositional to Jeannie.

The episode "Jeannie or the Tiger?" begins with Tony and his mother in a phone conversation. Jeannie asks him about the conversation, and he tells her that they just talked about the usual things: "stay out of drafts, marry a nice girl." Jeannie responds that she is a nice girl, and Tony says, "Yes, you are a nice girl; however, I don't think you're what my mother has in mind." Jeannie then reflects on the fact that she has had little contact with her own family and that she hasn't seen her sister Jeannie in over 200 years. Tony asks, "Jeannie? Your sister's name is Jeannie?" Jeannie answers, "Oh, yes, we are all Jeannies," and Tony appropriately inquires, "How do you tell you all apart?" Jeannie's response lays the foundation for the twins functioning as binary oppositions. She says, "You will have no difficulty telling my sister apart from me, Master. She's very different." Jeannie doesn't mention their physical similarities; rather, she remains focused on their differences as people. In the episode "Tony's Wife," written by Christopher Golato (a pen name for Sheldon), Jeannie is told she must go away and is determined to find her replacement for Tony first. She believes she knows what type of woman will make Tony happy, a type that is surprising because Jeannie's requirements involve a great deal of "formal education"—something Jeannie herself doesn't have. In the episode, Sister Jeannie pops in while Jeannie is reading a book, saying, "I've come to warn you. You've got to get out of here." Jeannie replies, "Get out of here? Why? I live here." Sister explains, "Have you read your zodiac sign? You're under the terrible sign of the Jinx. Everything you do for the next 15 years is going to be disastrous." Sister tells Jeannie that if she stays around Tony, she is going to destroy him and that it is in his best interest that she return to Baghdad for 15 years, in order to protect him. Jeannie decides that, before she leaves, she must find another female partner for Tony. She asks Helen Wheeler over to have dinner with Tony. When he asks why, Jeannie tells him that she is trying to find him a girlfriend, saying, "She's pretty and she can cook and sew. And she likes children, is a former Miss Cocoa Beach, and has a 'mistress' degree from the University of Florida." Jeannie calls her degree a "mistress degree" because she would call a female master "mistress"; so she assumes that when a woman earns a master's degree, it must be called a "mistress degree." Unfortunately, though, this dialogue indicates there is more going on here. Jeannie is not educated; she loves to serve in the domestic sphere; she is willing to either use or not use her powers according to Tony's wishes;

she is physically beautiful; she is dependent and naïve; and she often misunderstands things in a way that makes her appear not only uneducated but ignorant. Yet, her idea of what Tony *should* like is somewhat of the complete opposite of Jeannie, yet able to cook and sew. We know from their marriage at the end of the series that Jeannie is indeed exactly what Tony wants—not some master's-degree-earning-beauty-queen—both attributes that position her to dominate the public sphere versus Jeannie, whose unbelievable powers must remain hidden in the private sphere. Incidentally, Helen Wheeler has far more in common with Sister Jeannie than with Jeannie, but Jeannie still believes these qualities are what Tony would want. Thus, her ignorance serves to endear her even more to Tony and potentially to us.

Finally, Jeannie is also aligned with natural domesticity, as she often attempts to cook or clean without her powers.[9] Sister is depicted as oppositional to service. The episode "Have You Ever Had a Genie Hate You,"[10] which was written by Allan Devon (another pen name for Sheldon), opens with Jeannie baking a cake. She pulls the cake out of the oven and says, "Oh, my master will love this." Sister Jeannie appears and makes the cake fall flat in center, thus serving in direct opposition to Jeannie's domestic efforts. Sister also emphasizes Jeannie's boring domestic life and lack of intellectual abilities, when she refers to Jeannie as her "square sister" or her "dumb little sister," as she does in "Genie, Genie, Who's Got the Genie?, Part 3" and "Have You Ever Had a Genie Hate You." In the "Have You Ever Had a Genie Hate You" episode, sister gives Jeannie a potion that makes her hate Tony and try to hurt him. Even Jeannie's methods for "evil," though, are couched in domesticity. To express her anger with Tony, she attempts to roast him, like a rotisserie chicken, on a rotating device in the oven. Even in her worst moments, Jeannie is aligned with goodness, innocence, service, and domesticity.

LOOSE INHIBITIONS

As with the other examples, *I Dream of Jeannie* depicts qualities of self-interest as selfishness in the evil-twin characters. More than any other doppelgänger analyzed in this study, Sister Jeannie (Sister) is perpetually depicted as needing to seduce men and steal them away from other women. Before discussing my analysis of the first Sister episode, "Jeannie or the Tiger?,"[11] I'd like to discuss briefly the episode's title. In this title, the tiger is obviously Jeannie's sister, and this is important because of the ways in which it connects to *Bewitched* treatments of Serena. Serena is always aligned with hunting, whether she is wearing a tiger fur coat or a pheasant feather boa; her identity as a hunter, a predator, is solidified by her attire. Here, in *I Dream of Jeannie*, we have a title that establishes Sister as a predator and the either/or, us/them mentality from the beginning. The title isn't "Jeannie and the Tiger." It is very intentionally "Jeannie *or* the Tiger," indicating their natural oppositions to each other. In this episode, Tony meets Sister for the first time. Jeannie blinks her in, and she arrives in blue smoke, connoting both her difference from Jeannie (whose smoke is pink) and her "masculine" desires—sex, career, assertiveness, etc. Sister appears, wearing a green version of Jeannie's costume, with excessive jewelry and makeup—associating sister Jeannie with excess, even in appearance. Sister is filing her nails, saying, "Yes, master Poopsie. What is it this time?" Jeannie tells her it is her sister, and they hug. Sister replies, "Oh, now careful, careful darling, my hair." Sister's primping and concern for beauty is overall depicted as being too concerned with herself and the judgments of others. She is self-absorbed and selfish.

Sister then sees a picture of Major Nelson and roars like a tiger, saying "groovy." She finds Tony so attractive that she decides, like a tiger, to go hunting and steal him from Jeannie. Posing as Jeannie, she meets Tony at the door of their home and kisses him aggressively (displaying her sexuality), dips him backward (displaying dominance), and again, roars like a tiger (displaying her predatory nature)—actions that, coming from the evil twin, imply a belief that women should not be the aggressors in sexual activity. This implication is validated by Tony's clear displeasure. He tells her to stop kissing him like that and to go to the kitchen and make dinner. However, as with most of the evil twins, the private sphere will not suffice for Sister: she wants a night out on the town and a gourmet meal they can both enjoy (that she doesn't have to cook). Much to Tony's frustration and anger, she blinks them to a fancy restaurant, and when they are finished, she orders him to pay the check so they can go dancing. In a statement that is intended to frustrate (potentially acknowledging Sheldon's finger on the pulse of feminist issues), Tony insists, "I give the orders around here. We are going home." Sister ignores this statement and blinks them to a disco-type dance club—much like Serena's Go-Go dancing scenes in *Bewitched*. Tony is trying to dance, when Sister says, "No, no darling; it's all in the hips. Watch." Tony responds, "I'm watching, I'm watching; you could get arrested for moves like that," and Sister says in a sexy tone, "For this? Oh, darling, you should see me when I really move." She then blinks them to an upscale dance club in Brazil, but Tony is falling asleep, asking, "Jeannie, can't we go home? I'm due at the base in 2 hours." Later in the episode, Sister blinks them to a tropical location, where they hunt a rhinoceros together—thus solidifying Sister's, like Serena's, association with the hunter, rather than the hunted.

Even though Tony is showing signs of exhaustion, claiming he has to work the next day, Sister disregards his needs and takes him dancing anyway. Consequently, Tony is too tired to work the next day. Sister's desires to travel and dance are not depicted as mere personal interests; they are portrayed as direct obstacles to Tony's ability to function effectively. Sister's desire for self-service is oppositional to and incompatible with Tony's need for service. This makes explicit Friedan's claim that the female desire for independence is regarded as evil, since it directly threatens the male's way of life—a way of life that depends upon the female putting his needs ahead of her own. The episode also depicts Sister seeking to function in the public sphere, and her need to dominate outside of the private sphere always causes conflict.

In the episode, "Have You Ever Had a Genie Hate You?," Sister brings Jeannie two lotions—one that she can sprinkle on Tony, so that he will fall instantly in love with her, and another to sprinkle on his enemies because, she says to Jeannie, "you must hate his enemies, and you are a terrible hater." Sister warns, "Just be sure not to get the flasks mixed up," but when Jeannie's back is turned, Sister switches the bottles. By this point, deceit is at the core of Sister's character. Her plan works momentarily, as Jeannie hates Tony and falls in love with his best friend, Roger Healey (Bill Daily). Later, Tony is sick in bed and Sister shows up to nurse him back to health. She tells him she wants to take him around the world, and Tony replies, "I'm an astronaut; not a playboy." Again, Sister's only reason for wanting Tony's health to improve is for her own sexual, worldly, and adventurous desires, which are presented in opposition to Tony's needs. Sister responds, "Don't be a drag, darling. You're going to have to give all that up. I hope you can samba." He sneezes. He asks her to leave him alone. She blinks him into a trendy, bright colorful shirt with psychedelic flowers and bright orange pants, saying, "Oh, kiss me Tony, baby." She grabs him by the large beaded necklace around his neck and kisses him aggressively. Once he leaves, she looks in the mirror, roars like a tiger, and says, as she primps her hair, "Oh, you're gorgeous." In the end, Tony pretends to be an old man, and his plan works. Sister no longer wants him because he can't "party" with her. Throughout, Sister is depicted as lacking self-control and desiring a life of excess in the public realm.

This excess is also displayed in "How to Marry an Astronaut." When Jeannie is frustrated that Tony won't marry her, Sister claims to be an expert on "hooking" a man. Jeannie asks her, "Do you know the right tricks?" Sister replies, "Well, I should. I've been married 47 times." She tells Jeannie to follow her process, and Jeannie asks if she is willing to get married again, just to instruct her. Sister says, "Sure. Forty-seven, 48, what's the difference?" Sister's indifference to respected institutions, such as marriage, serves to add another layer to her life of excess. In fact, her plan for hooking Major Healy involves further excess—she blinks him excessive luxury items, such as a Rolls Royce and a yacht, all while faking the domestic activities of sewing buttons and cooking meals. Thus, she is persistently focused on her appearance—a focus on self instead of others—wants to travel the world, dance and party all night, seduce Tony, and marry 48 times—all activities that connote a life of excess.

INTELLECTUAL PROWESS

To return to the episode "Have You Ever Had a Jeannie Hate You," Sister decides to leave, saying, "I'm going where the action is. Serves me right for having such a dumb sister." Sister claims that Jeannie prefers a quiet life of service over "going where the action is," and labels her as "dumb," while the alter ego, whom the show depicts as both oppositional and evil, regards herself as more intelligent. A more compelling example of "intellectual prowess" is in the episode "Operation: First Couple on the Moon."[12] NASA is interviewing women to accompany Tony on a trip to the moon. Tony claims he wants to get out of it because "who wants to go to the moon with a female Louis Pasteur? Have you seen these lady scientists? Forget it." Tony's dialogue states explicitly that education in women is considered unattractive and unfeminine. Friedan argued that the more a woman's "intelligence exceeds [her] job requirements, the greater [her] boredom," so Tony's dialogue can also be interpreted as a reflection of male fears of housewife boredom.[13] As more women became educated, according to Friedan, more became bored with housewifery—something many males perceived as a threat to their comfortable existence on the home front. Sister, playing a "female Louis Pasteur" in this episode, embodies these fears precisely, and as the oppositional alter ego, aligns these qualities with the evil side of the Friedan split.

Sister establishes her intellectual superiority explicitly in the episode "How to Marry an Astronaut."[14] Jeannie is reading *Bride* magazine in her bottle, when Sister shows up and traps her there. Jeannie says, "You let me out of here, or I'll tell mama." Sister tells her she was joking and joins her in the bottle, saying, "I wanted to know what was going on with that gorgeous master of yours. Are you married yet?" Jeannie says they are not, and she doesn't understand why because she reads all the magazines and follows their instructions. Sister suggests a love potion, but Jeannie wants Tony to marry her of his own free will. Sister replies, "Sis, wake up. No man gets married of his own free will. They have to be led, persuaded, cajoled. You have to dangle a carrot in front of their nose." Missing her sister's point, Jeannie responds, "Oh, but my master does not like carrots." Sister says, "Darling, you can make a man eat shredded cardboard if you know the right tricks. Just to show you there are no hard feelings, I'm going to give you a personalized course in how to marry a man. I'm going to go after a man and let you watch and see how I hook him. And you can take notes on what I do." Sister establishes herself as both instructor of Jeannie and dominator of men.

Returning to the episode "Have You Ever Had a Genie Hate You," Sister provides Jeannie with love and hate lotions, but she switches the bottles so that Jeannie unknowingly sprinkles Tony with the hate lotion and Roger with the love lotion. This leaves Tony available for Sister to try to steal him away, and she says, "I can't wait to start training you. How you ever stood that square sister of mine, I'll never know. She and Major Healey deserve each other." Tony asks her how she accomplished this trickery, and she admits that she switched the magic lotions. Tony replies, "You're much smarter than Jeannie," and Sister says, "Oh, I'm the greatest." Jeannie is perpetually depicted as naïve and called dumb, stupid, and square by her sister, while Sister persistently claims to know more than those around her. Her intelligence is depicted as manipulation throughout the series.

CAREER INTERESTS

I Dream of Jeannie engages and responds to *The Feminine Mystique* through evil-twin depictions of career interests, as well. In the episode "Jeannie-Go-Round,"[15] Sister is trying to steal Tony again, and part of this involves discrediting Jeannie in the eyes of Tony and his supervisor, Dr. Bellows (Hayden Rorke). Posing as Jeannie,

Sister convinces Dr. Bellows to allow an entertainer for "the boys." She then puts a spell on the hired performer and takes the stage herself, performing a song and dance number. Instead of sitting contently by Tony's side, as Jeannie would, Sister displays a desire to be accomplished, noticed, and applauded, to have her talents utilized in the public sphere—qualities ascribed to the evil side of the Friedan split because they threaten to take away or distract from the male character's existence.

A more powerful example exists in the episode "Operation: First Couple on the Moon."[16] As mentioned earlier, Tony is going to the moon with a woman. Jeannie asks why he didn't tell her, and he indicates that he is trying to get out of the project, asking again, "who wants to go to the moon with a female Louis Pasteur?" Sister appears and tells Jeannie she is surprised that she fell for Tony's "Louis Pasteur line." This causes Jeannie to be jealous and ask, "You mean my master will be living on the moon with a beautiful woman?" Sister comforts Jeannie by telling her that she will handle the situation. With Jeannie's trust, Sister pretends to be a female scientist, who wins a spot to go with Tony to the moon. Eventually, Jeannie discovers her sister's real motives (to steal Tony, as usual). Sister demeans her, saying, "Don't be such a square, sister. The moon is a dull lump of clay. The real swinging planet is Venus." Sister proceeds to train for the mission with Tony, all the while continuing to seduce him. Eventually, Tony becomes aware of Sister's antics and captures her in a tube. But unlike Sister, when Jeannie attempts to replace her on the project (i.e., function in the public sphere), things go wrong, and they must cancel the entire mission.

POLITICAL INTERESTS

In returning to "Genie, Genie, Who's Got the Genie?, Part 3," Sister disguises herself as a maid at NASA headquarters. Tony has been given an assignment to relocate to Panama and Ecuador, areas near the equator, while his colleague has been assigned an area in the Middle East, but Sister switches the locations of these assignments. When Sister goes to tell Jeannie goodbye, as she prepares to join Tony in the Middle East, she says, "I have just arranged for my master to be assigned to the Middle East, and I wouldn't dream of being apart from my master . . . my new master, Major Nelson. Once I get him on my home turf in Baghdad, he's going to have a hard time helping himself." I'm identifying this as political interests because Sister's desires are depicted as going beyond the willingness to be with Tony in Cocoa Beach—on *his* turf; she is depicted as needing the type of power and control over Tony that only the comfort and governance of her own country can provide.

ASSERTIVENESS

In "Jeannie or the Tiger?," Sister is again attempting to steal Tony away from Jeannie. In order to do so, though, she needs to manufacture a plan for Jeannie to remain out of her way, so she decides to trap her. Connivingly, she tells Jeannie that her bottle appears too small for comfort, so naïvely, Jeannie transfers herself into the bottle to show her how cozy it is. Then, as Sister traps her in the bottle, Sister says, "Glad you like it, darling, because now it's home sweet home. And don't worry about your Major Nelson; I'm going to take good care of him." Sister then blinks herself into Jeannie's clothes, but she adds excessive jewelry to the outfit. When Roger discovers that Jeannie is trapped in the bottle, Sister blinks him to various remote locations, including the arctic. Things escalate, as Tony begins to ascertain the truth. Sister tells Jeannie that if she wants him, she is going to have to fight for him. She and Jeannie hurl objects at each other, but these objects ultimately hit Tony. Eventually, Tony is hung by his pants from the rhino head on the wall, to serve in tandem with the rhino as "the hunted," while Sister remains the hunter. Sister's assertiveness has left Tony literally hanging by his pants.

Sister asserts herself again in "Tony's Wife," when she pops in to deliver a warning to Jeannie, saying, "I've come to warn you. You've got to get out of here. Have you read your zodiac sign? You're under the terrible sign of the Jinx. Everything you do for the next 15 years is going to be disastrous." Sister tells her that if she stays around Tony, she is going to destroy him and that it is in his best interest that she returns to Baghdad for 15 years to protect him. Jeannie's first thought is not about her own well-being, but about Tony's, so she decides to find Tony a wife before she leaves. As I've mentioned, she invites over Helen Wheeler for dinner in an effort to pair them before her requisite departure.

Similarly, in the episode "Genie, Genie, Who's Got the Genie?, Part 3,"[17] Sister overhears that Jeannie is locked in a safe at NASA headquarters, so she blinks herself there. Sister notifies Jeannie of her presence, and Jeannie asks her if she is going to help her get out of here. Sister answers, "I'd love to, darling, but there is this little thing called sibling rivalry." In a question that could also indicate Jeannie's intellectual inferiority, she asks, "What is sibling rivalry?" Sister responds, "Well, my square sister; it means you've got something I want. And with you locked up in that cozy little safe, there isn't anything to keep me from getting it." Naïvely, Jeannie asks what Sister wants. "Well, it's about six foot one, and he's got lovely brown hair, big blue eyes . . ." Jeannie realizes that she is indicating that she wants Tony, so Jeannie says, "I would rather stay in here forever." Sister, asserting her authority, replies, "Your wish is my command. Ciao." She locks Jeannie in the safe and leaves.

This episode is interesting because it provides a situation where the sisters do not have equal powers. Jeannie's wish involves sacrifice—she is willing to give up her freedom so that Tony doesn't become her sister's manservant—and Sister programs that sacrifice for her own desires. Regardless, Tony follows his new assignment to Baghdad and begins looking for a genie named Haji, who can release Jeannie from the safe. While Tony is in the Baghdad market, the locals try to pick his pockets and swindle him—another example of the orientalism of the series—but Sister, disguised completely in a red dress and veil (colors that, like Serena in *Bewitched*, serve to associate the twin with the colors of hell), tells Tony that if he wants to find

Haji, he should follow her. They arrive in a room with five women, and Sister tells Tony it is her master's harem. Tony recognizes her as Sister, and he tells her that she has to help him get Jeannie out of the safe. Sister replies, "Of course, darling, when I've gotten tired of you after 20 or 30 years." Then, she traps Tony in a bird cage. She says, "Don't lose your cool, Major, baby. I'll protect you." As is typical, Sister assumes stereotypical "masculine" qualities, such as offering Tony protection, being strong, and maintaining control. However, prior to this episode, when Sister dons the red harem outfit, her desire to have Tony is depicted more as sexual desire and less about wanting to trap and control him. Once Sister is wearing the red, though, her typical motivations of seduction—something, I argue, is only depicted as evil because a woman is doing it—turn to the actual evil intentions of power, kidnapping, and entrapment.

Tony is eventually demasculinized into begging the women to release him, but they refuse. He tells them he is hungry and needs to be fed—trying to appeal to their nurturing sides. His begging doesn't work, and he attempts to infantilize Sister, saying, "Look here, young lady. I don't think you understand that I'm here on official business. When NASA hears that I'm missing, they're going to send someone to look for me." Sister replies, "I'm sure they will, but frankly, darling, I don't think they'll be looking in a Baghdad harem in a birdcage." She asserts her parental-type authority by placing a sheet over the cage and saying, "nighty night." Eventually, Roger arrives in Baghdad to find Tony, and Sister cages him with Tony, saying, "Oh don't worry, my pets. In a year or two, if you are very good boys, I'll get you separate cages." All of Sister's dialogue condescends to them from an assumed position of power. Even though the kidnapping and caging enacted by Sister in this episode could be interpreted as evil—not just a desire for a sense of separate self—the impetus for the caging is assertiveness and sexual desire. Sister identifies what she wants and pursues it. Her desires appear to change from seduction to entrapment only once she is depicted in red, as evil, and once she is on her own turf, indicating power.

This episode aligns Sister with evil rather explicitly. Sister's master eventually returns, and she says that she expected him to be on an extended vacation. He says that with a genie like her, he can't risk an extended vacation. He asks, "What mischief have you been up to?" He discovers the men in the birdcage, looks at her, and knows immediately that she needs to be punished. This implies that this behavior is typical for Sister, and even among her fellow genies, she is known for her mischief. However, when she is in Jeannie's world—not Baghdad—her behavior is less like mischief and more like assertiveness and a hunger for power. Her behavior is depicted as becoming actual evil once she is in Baghdad.

In "My Sister, the Homewrecker,"[18] Sister finds out that Tony and Jeannie are married and decides to break up the marriage. As usual, Sister wants Tony for herself. Jeannie tells her she is a "one-man woman," and Sister responds, "Ha, sister; your reputation is about to be changed." That evening, Sister poses as Jeannie and corners Biff Jelico (played by Eden's husband at the time, Michael Ansara), a handsome astronaut that all the women at the party are attempting to attract, in the garden.

She doesn't wait for him to make the first move; she begins kissing him passionately. Jelico believes that evening that he has fallen in love, so when Tony invites him over for dinner to meet his Jeannie (the actual Jeannie), Jelico believes Jeannie has been cheating on Tony with him (he has actually been seduced by Sister posing as Jeannie). Sister pops in again, disguises herself as Jeannie and says, "Now this is going to be interesting." Sister's desires are always depicted as being good for her but bad for everyone else, which could also be said of the public perception of feminism in the sixties.

CONCLUSIONS

Like Serena and Patty, Sister is depicted as possessing that unacceptable flaw of not finding contentment in the private sphere and wanting to function in and dominate the public sphere, which sixties television implies is not her proper place. From the beginning, Sister is the hunter, not the hunted. She is depicted as a predator with an intense sexual appetite. In fact, in that first episode, "Jeannie or the Tiger," Sister actually leads Tony on a hunt. She blinks them to the desert to hunt a rhino; to confirm the dangers of Sister functioning like this in masculine roles in the public sphere, the rhino is what takes Tony down in the end. The hunted rhino's head has been taxidermized and placed on Tony's wall. At the end of the episode, when Sister begins fighting with Jeannie over Tony, Sister flings him into the air, hooking him by his pants on the rhino's horn. He is literally left hanging by the seat of his pants, and this is the disastrous result of Sister's attempt to function in the male-dominated public sphere. Sister's character evolves over the five seasons, but the earlier episodes, especially, strongly support my claims here that she is depicted as evil only because she is sexual, career-minded, intelligent, political, and assertive, and desires a sense of separate self, in general, when the social norms say that an acceptable woman is submissive, servile, domesticated, and dependent.

Furthermore, Sister's constant primping serves to further her depiction as a woman living a life of excess. Sister is not desiring to look good just for her master, as Jeannie does in the private realm and as would be acceptable by social norms of the sixties. Sister primps to look good for men she pursues in the public realm, which places her on the evil side of the split. In every episode, Sister is filing her nails, checking her hair, avoiding anything that will potentially disturb her beauty (e.g., hugging Jeannie), and wearing excessive jewelry and makeup—an indication that she is not only vain but "high maintenance." Sister is perpetually portrayed as desiring a life of excess—makeup, jewelry, sex, dancing, dining—a depiction that coincides with the show's implication that Sister is an unhappy woman because she is a selfish woman.

As the series progressed, though, Sister's motives did tend to evolve from initially serving to align her character with feminism to eventually being depicted as actual evil. Surely, this is the result of multiple writers and evolving audiences. Eden also commented on the show's reception and connection to feminism:

Down the line, when the feminist movement swept America, the critics also lambasted the show for depicting a master-slave relationship that they claimed was an insult to liberated women everywhere. I always considered that to be nonsense. *I Dream of Jeannie* is a fantasy, a modern-day fairy tale that has nothing to do with women's liberation. The show's purpose was not to make a political statement but simply to entertain audiences, which is what it indisputably succeeded in doing. *I Dream of Jeannie* genuinely delved into the battle of the sexes, but in a cute way . . . For despite the surface elements ("Yes, Master," and so on), it was Jeannie who dominated Major Nelson, not the reverse.

I both agree and disagree with Eden here. The criticism regarding the master-slave relationship is valid and is a primary reason I began researching the show in the beginning. It bothered me that much of the feminist commentary focused on the "Yes-Master" aspect of the show, ignoring the richness of other aspects of the show. In fact, the master-slave relationship between Jeannie and Tony is what made the show appealing: as Eden acknowledges, we all knew who was actually in charge—Jeannie. I do, however, feel strongly that the show reflected an awareness of the national feminist discourse, even beyond its use of an evil twin. In fact, as I've mentioned, my first foray into *I Dream of Jeannie* scholarship analyzed representations of "supernatural housework" and how they connected Jeannie to Friedan's claim that, in an effort to justify her existence, the mid-century housewife found herself expanding the housework to fill the time.[6] In that project, I argue that Jeannie (in addition to Samantha from *Bewitched* and Morticia from *The Addams Family*) has the ability to make the vacuum cleaner run on its own, and sometimes she chooses this option. But just as real mid-century housewives weren't always choosing easier, time-saving methods for their housework, "television housewives with supernatural abilities weren't either. They were *choosing* to be typical housewives, and if typical housewives wash their own dishes and sew their own dresses, then they want to do the same, even if it takes all day. A high regard for normalcy and status quo is highlighted throughout these shows,"[19] whether it is through domestic activity or Jeannie demanding, "No more presto . . . I want to be a typical woman."[20] Thus, I have always regarded the *Jeannie* series as being in conversation with feminism—even if it was not the show's purpose—and my good/evil-twin analysis furthers this assertion.

Eden mentions throughout her autobiography what it was like to work with Larry Hagman, and one of her anecdotes involved his displeasure that Eden was playing Jeannie in such a cute way. Hagman was apparently receiving pushback from viewers about how mean his character is to someone who is so "little and cute." To appease Hagman, Sheldon asked Eden to play Jeannie as a stronger woman, so that Hagman didn't always look like such a bad guy. Eden filmed the next two episodes as a much more willful Jeannie, but when these episodes were shown to a focus group, not a single member of the group liked the stronger Jeannie. Consequently, they had to dub a "sweeter" voice over Eden's in those two episodes. The audience's insistence that Jeannie be good sets the stage for the existence of an evil twin. If Jeannie had been "acerbic and willful," as Eden claims to have made the "stronger Jeannie," she would have embodied too many of the qualities that belong on the evil side of the split—qualities that audiences had been programmed to dislike and that Sister touted proudly. This fact is underscored by the 1985 NBC television movie *I Dream of Jeannie: 15 Years Later*. The plot for this sequel involved a new liberated and more assertive Jeannie—a personality a bit like the one Eden attempted to create in the earlier "stronger Jeannie" at Sheldon's request. Jeannie and Tony have a son (played by Mackenzie Astin, the son of Patty Duke and John Astin), but Jeannie feels unappreciated—much like Natalie in *The Patty Duke* episode "Are Mother's People?"—so she moves out and rents her own apartment. Since Jeannie's character now embodies many of the attributes that sixties television had placed on the evil side of the split— a desire for independence, in general (Jeannie was even allowed to show her belly button)—in order for Sister Jeannie to function effectively, she must display actual evil, which she does.

Ultimately, Eden finds Jeannie, the character, to be pure fantasy and the show to be mere entertainment. She is right, but it is also the ways in which the series interacted with reality that made it so special. If its purpose was to be pure fantasy, the show wouldn't have worked so diligently to maintain certain elements of reality, like bringing in a UCLA professor to teach Eden how to speak Persian properly for the pilot episode. It was the combination of fantasy, attention to details of reality, and a focus on real social issues, public or private, that made the show so special. Plus, it was fun. Even though *I Dream of Jeannie* was never an "industry sweetheart," Jeannie and her evil sister have always been enormously popular with fans,[21] and Eden even admits to loving her opportunities to play the sister "because, as they say, the devil always gets the best lines."[22]

NOTES

1. Jenny Peters, "The gentleman preferred a blonde" in *Variety* February 20–26, 2006, B4.

2. Barbara Eden, *Jeannie, Out of the Bottle* (New York: Three Rivers Press, 2011), 115.

3. *I Dream of Jeannie*, season 1, episode 5, "G. I. Jeannie," written by Bill Davenport, directed by Alan Rafkin, October 1965.

4. Barbara Eden, *Jeannie, Out of the Bottle*, 120.

5. Ibid., 132.

6. *I Dream of Jeannie*, season 1, episode 4, "Jeannie and the Marriage Caper," written by Tom Waldman and Frank Waldman, October 1965.

7. Sarah Kornfield, "The E-man-ci-pation of Jeannie: Feminist Doppelgangers on U.S. Television," in *Communication, Culture & Critique*, 445.

8. *I Dream of Jeannie*, season 1, episode 9, "Moving Finger," written by Harry Essex and Jerry Seelan, directed by Gene Nelson, October 1965.

9. She also admits, though, in certain episodes, such as "My Turned On Master," that she "is a terrible cook without her powers."

10. *I Dream of Jeannie*, season 3, episode 24, "Have You Ever Had a Genie Hate You," written by Allan Devon, directed by Claudio Guzman, March 1968.

11. *I Dream of Jeannie*, season 3, episode 3, "Jeannie or the Tiger," written by James Henerson, directed by Hal Cooper, September 1967.

12. *I Dream of Jeannie*, season 3, episode 25, "Operation: First Couple on the Moon," written by Arthur Julian, directed by Claudio Guzman, March 1968.

13. Friedan, *Feminine Mystique*, 251.

14. *I Dream of Jeannie*, season 4, episode 10, "How to Marry an Astronaut," written by James Henerson, directed by Hal Cooper, December 1968.

15. *I Dream of Jeannie*, season 4, episode 24, "Jeannie-Go-Round," written by James Henerson, directed by Claudio Guzman, April 1969.

16. *I Dream of Jeannie*, season 3, episode 25, "Operation: First Couple on the Moon," written by Arthur Julian, directed by Claudio Guzman, March 1968.

17. *I Dream of Jeannie*, season 3, episode 18, "Genie, Genie, Who's Got the Genie?, Part 3" written by James Henerson, directed by Hal Cooper, January 1968.

18. *I Dream of Jeannie*, season 5, episode 12, "My Sister, the Home Wrecker," written by James Henerson, directed by Claudio Guzman, December 1969.

19. Humphreys, "Supernatural Housework," 112.

20. This occurs in the episode "The Americanization of Jeannie," 1965.

21. The series has had such longevity that they filmed *I Dream of Jeannie: 15 Years Later* and *I Still Dream of Jeannie*, an NBC movie of the week in 1985.

22. Eden, *Jeannie, Out of the Bottle*, 227.

4

Gilligan's Island, The Brady Bunch, and *Doctor Who*

This chapter combines the analyses of three series: *Gilligan's Island, The Brady Bunch,* and *Doctor Who.* Unlike *Bewitched,* which had 22 episodes featuring evil cousin Serena, *The Patty Duke Show,* which had all episodes featuring twin cousins, and *I Dream of Jeannie,* which had 9 episodes featuring the evil sister Jeannie, *Gilligan's Island, The Brady Bunch,* and *Doctor Who* each had only one female evil-twin episode; thus, they have been combined in this chapter to underscore not only the prevalence and popularity of the twinning trope in the 1960s, but also to serve as examples of the similarities among all American female evil-twin treatments in this decade. *Doctor Who* serves as a non-American example, to illustrate the differences between an evil American twin depiction and an evil non-American twin depiction.

Gilligan's Island and *The Brady Bunch* were both created and produced by Sherwood Schwartz, who collaborated with Sol Saks, creator of *Bewitched,* on multiple projects. These five popular series were created by just three individuals, all of whom shared the same professional circles. *Gilligan's Island* aired for three seasons, from 1964–1967, and the premise of the show is creative, to say the least. Seven castaways, Gilligan (Bob Denver), The Skipper (Alan Hale, Jr.), Ginger (Tina Louise), the professor (Russell Johnson), Mary Ann (Dawn Wells), and Mr. and Mrs. Thurston Howell III (Jim Backus and Natalie Schafer), are shipwrecked on an uncharted island. They encounter various individuals who have also found themselves shipwrecked on the island, and they make many attempts to be rescued. In his autobiography, *Inside Gilligan's Island: From Creation to Syndication,* Schwartz maintains that he chose these characters deliberately and is aware of the social content of the show—he claims to have conceived of the island as a social microcosm.[1] Academics and fans alike have noticed these deeper implications of the show. For example, Cantor wrote *Gilligan Unbound: Pop Culture in the Age of Globalization,* claiming that *Gilligan's Island* served a more significant purpose than mere entertainment—it served to herald American democracy. He says, "The Skipper embodies American military might, the Professor represents American science and technological know-how, and the Millionaire reflects the power of American business . . . the presence of The Movie Star among the castaways even hints at the source of America's cultural domination of the world—Hollywood."[2] Regarding Gilligan's position in this democracy, Cantor says, "Representing the average citizen at his most ordinary, Gilligan presides over a kind of democratic utopia on the island and is repeatedly called upon to act as its savior."[3] Cantor's assessment reflects what Schwartz always knew: the show represented more than silly, slapstick entertainment. This is also why, as Catherine Seipp reveals, "bumbling, unsophisticated Gilligan has a way of ruining the plans of every Soviet cosmonaut or Third World dictator who drops by."[4] This observation comments upon the twinning trope used in an episode discussed in the Introduction, "Gilligan vs Gilligan," where Gilligan's twin is a Soviet spy—an example that confirms the depth of the series' social commentary.[5]

Like *I Dream of Jeannie*, the show's critical reviews weren't always favorable. For example, writing for *The New York Times*, Jack Gould claimed the show was "quite possibly the most preposterous situation comedy of the season." But it was a huge hit with audiences, both in the 1960s and in syndication. Schwartz said that by the time of the publication of his autobiography, "The episodes of *Gilligan's Island* [had] been repeated more often in more places than any other television series in history."[6] Although it was not an industry favorite, the original series displayed remarkable longevity and inspired multiple TV movies—three, to be exact—in addition to two animated series. The series has maintained remarkable long-term popularity; Cantor even describes it as "the most successful bad show in the history of television."[7]

GILLIGAN'S ISLAND'S "ALL ABOUT EVA" SYNOPSIS

In the episode "All About Eva," written by Joanna Lee, Tina Louise plays dual roles as Ginger and an identical woman named Eva. The title alone foreshadows the dynamics between Ginger and Eva, as it alludes to the famous film *All About Eve*—a 1950 American film about a young, adoring fan (Anne Baxter) attempting to assume the persona and life of a Broadway star (Bette Davis). In this episode, Eva arrives on the island and is first seen throwing her suitcase ashore (indicating her plans to stay) and tying up her boat. Much of her appearance aligns with the other evil-twin depictions. She has dark, black hair and wears a dark brown skirt suit, glasses, hose, and black pumps. Her outfit makes her appear to have come from a professional situation back home. Gilligan and Ginger are the first of the castaways to spot the boat, and after gathering the others, everyone assumes the woman and her boat must be a rescue mission, so they don't understand why they can't find a radio on the boat. Gilligan then finds footsteps and thinks it is a "beast." The professor also sees them and remarks, "those are the footprints of a woman." The professor finds one of Eva's shoes in the sand. Skipper immediately shouts how they need to find her because she

Figure 4.1.   Alan Hale Jr. as the Skipper, Tina Louise as Ginger, and Bob Denver as Gilligan in *Gilligan's Island*, PictureLux / The Hollywood Archives / Alamy Stock Photo

will have a key to the boat. To further this Cinderella plotline, Gilligan asks, "If we find her, we don't know what she looks like, so how will we know it's her?" Skipper responds, "Let's put it this way. She's the one with the single shoe."

They eventually find the woman wearing one shoe, Eva, and they are surprised that she is willing to give them her boat. She begins crying and tells them her name is Eva Grubb. Gilligan attempts to console her, saying, "That's not too great a name

but you always can change it." Eva tells them why she is running away from civilization: "Because I never want to see another human being for as long as I live, particularly not a man. Men don't even know I exist. All through school not a boy even
looked at me. Finally, ten days ago, I had my first date—a blind date—and just ten
minutes after meeting me, he suddenly developed a headache and had to go home. I
saved up all my money to buy that boat, so that I could find a deserted island. I
wanted to be alone. I guess I picked the wrong one."

Gilligan tells her that they would be happy to desert the island for her, and she
gives them the key to the boat, claiming she will never return to civilization. Gilligan and others take Eva to meet the Thurstons, and they immediately ask her if
she is related to the Grubbs they knew back home—a family who had an engaged
daughter. Eva gets upset again, crying, "I've never been engaged to anyone, and I
never will be. I gave you the key to the boat. The least you could do is not to mention men." The castaways all agree that they shouldn't leave Eva on the island in
this emotional state, so they secretly make a plan to send the boat back to get her,
once they have returned to civilization. Eva finds out about the plan and removes
the spark plugs from the boat so that it can't be used. They decide they must do
something to make Eva *want* to return to civilization. Mary Ann asks, "Why would
she want to go home? It's just going to be the same as when she left . . . no dates, no
boyfriend." Ginger agrees, "No wonder! She's so plain. She doesn't do anything to
make herself more attractive." They decide that making Eva beautiful will make her
want to return home, so they organize an Eva makeover. Ginger says, "Goodbye,
ugly duckling. Hello, beautiful swan!"

Ginger and Mary Ann give Eva a makeover, and with lighter hair, she ends up
looking like Ginger's identical twin. The same twin dialogue we have encountered in
other examples occurs in this scene. Mary Ann exclaims, "You two are exactly alike!"
Mrs. Thurston says, "It's remarkable; you could be twin brothers," and the professor
shouts, "Good heavens; two Gingers!" Eva doesn't believe that, even with her new
look, men will be attracted to her, so they send her out to flirt with Gilligan. She sits
next to Gilligan, as he remarks how much she looks like Ginger. Eva replies, "But
I'm not Ginger. I'm me." She then attempts to seduce Gilligan, without taking his
hints that he is not interested, and she begins kissing him passionately and sitting on
his lap. To further Eva's seductiveness in her new role, when Gilligan tells the group
about what she did, they ask if she really turned it on. Gilligan replies, "All I can say
is that I couldn't turn her off."

Eva decides she indeed wants to go home, and everyone celebrates. Then, Eva
overhears a conversation between Mary Ann and Ginger regarding whether Eva will
actually be happy back home. Ginger says she doesn't think so because to be attractive, she would need the confidence and poise of Ginger Grant, but there is only one
Ginger Grant. Ginger suspects Eva will go back to being just Eva Grubb. Eva gets the
idea to assume Ginger's identity and return to civilization with the other castaways
to take over Ginger's career. Eva meets with Ginger, bonks her over the head with a
coconut wrapped in a scarf, and ties her up. She reveals her plan to leave Ginger on

the island, saying to Ginger, "Bye Eva. Sorry you can't come to the party tonight. I'll explain that you're all tied up."

That night, Eva goes back and forth, pretending to be both Eva and Ginger at the party, until the real Ginger shows up, telling the others that "Our little Cinderella conked me on the head; she tied me up and she was going to leave me here while she went back and resumed my career." Eva admits that the excitement of being beautiful for the first time made her a little crazy and she is ashamed of herself. She apologizes and asks for their forgiveness. They all decide to return home the next morning, but Eva sails away overnight, leaving only a note indicating that she realized she was a good actress during that fake apology and that she is returning to civilization to be the new Ginger Grant.

"ALL ABOUT EVA" ANALYSIS

The episode establishes Eva as Ginger's dark-haired opposite from the beginning, and in the moment Gilligan finds her shoe, we understand that Eva is going to receive a Cinderella treatment, as they search for the woman to whom the shoe belongs. The episode surprises us, though, when our Cinderella is not only *not* looking for a man, she claims never to want to see a man ever again. In a strange twist, Eva is both unhappy because men reject her, indicating that, like Cinderella, she would like to fall in love with one, while simultaneously professing to hate men, which is reminiscent of the "man-hating" feminist stereotype of the sixties. Consequently, as a self-proclaimed man-hater with dark hair, wearing a professional suit, we immediately align Eva with the evil side of the split. Then, she announces that her last name is "Grubb," which could mean a couple of things. Eva's name indicates she is like a grub, a maggot, which feeds off of others, much like Eva plans to feed off of Ginger's success. It could also mean she is grubby, contemptable; a person who is comfortable with deceit would also be worthy of such a name. Nevertheless, we understand that Eva is not going to be a typical Cinderella, even though her transformation goes from simple, plain, and under the control of others to beautiful, confident, and in control of her future.

Eva's dialogue continues to perpetuate her disdain for men, which is similar to Serena's and Sister's treatment of men when they don't get to have their ways with them (e.g., Serena turns Darrin into a gorilla and Sister traps Tony in a cage). The same is true for Eva. Men have not responded to her advances the way she had hoped, but since she does not possess magical powers, she chooses isolation as a way to deal with rejection. She is a nuanced evil twin in this way, but the similarities still exist. The episode makes one thing clear: non-beautiful women cannot possibly be happy in American society, according to contemporary social norms. Eva's entire unhappiness is based on the fact that men are not attracted to her. *Gilligan's Island* provides our first example of an "unattractive" evil twin, something that will connect Eva in this episode with Emma in the *Brady Bunch* episode. Eva's lack of desirability makes it difficult for her to maintain the "loose inhibitions" of the other evil twin, as she is not attractive enough to be seductive. However, her first post-makeover action is to seduce Gilligan, which aligns her character with the loose inhibitions established by previous evil twins. Without his consent, Eva dominates Gilligan, turning his head toward her, kissing him passionately, and pulling herself onto his lap. She has already established her control and sexual desire. Much like the other evil twins, Eva is depicted as being very comfortable with deceit. The castaways are kind enough to accept her apology, so we are surprised to find out that it was a part of Eva's plan. Her deceit and victorious ruse mean that she displays qualities of both loose inhibition (lying) and intellectual prowess (effective trickery).

For career interests, Eva is depicted as a professional woman, even though we do not know her career precisely. The hose she is wearing seems to be the strongest piece of evidence, as she is contrasted with all of the other women on the island because she is clearly wearing hose in the heat of a "deserted" island. Since we know she didn't come straight from her disappointing date (which she claims occurred ten days prior), we assume she must need to dress like this on an average day, which would likely identify her as a career woman. Also, once she realizes the potential of assuming Ginger's Hollywood career—note that Eva's existence places Ginger on the good side of the split, which indicates why she cannot have career interests anymore and why Eva must assume those interests in the end—she is willing to injure and abandon, just to secure the spotlighted career for herself.

Eva's glasses, hair bun, and suit align her early on with intellect, or at least serious-ness. She also speaks in a low, authoritative tone—which functions in opposition to Ginger's whispery, Marilyn-Monroe-type tone. She appears educated, simply through the precise way that she speaks, but she is further depicted as intelligent in the various ways she successfully schemes, from removing the boat's spark plugs to ultimately taking over Ginger's career. Finally, Eva asserts herself, even before her transformation. She is straightforward with the castaways about her needs, and then when those needs change, she has no problem asserting herself again. Even though she does actually engage in violence, which is something more typical of the male evil twins mentioned in the Introduction, the female-twin violence is still depicted differently. When Gilligan had a twin in "Gilligan vs. Gilligan," the twin actually attempted to kill Gilligan, first with a pocket knife and then with a boulder. His goal was to "get rid of" Gilligan, and his method is attempted murder, which would indicate actual evil. Although Eva's plans are nefarious, she makes it clear that she only wants to restrain Ginger until she can get away; thus, she uses a wrapped coco-nut, versus a knife or boulder, to subdue Ginger. The supposed evil in female twins still remains very different from male depictions, even in this example. Like other examples, Eva's ultimate flaw is her need to dominate the public sphere—something she desires so intently that she leaves the castaways stranded. Since her career inter-ests must stand in opposition to Ginger for the good/evil-twin formula to work, Eva's claiming of a Hollywood career simultaneously strips Ginger of hers.

THE BRADY BUNCH'S "SERGEANT EMMA" SYNOPSIS

As mentioned, *The Brady Bunch* was also created by Sherwood Schwartz, and its example of female twinning bears some resemblance to the "All About Eva" episode of *Gilligan's Island*, even though this episode was written by Harry Winkler, not Sherwood Schwartz. This indicates that the use of the twinning trope to reflect and produce the split in the American woman's image was firmly established by now. *The Brady Bunch* aired for five seasons (1969–1974) on the ABC network and became an enduring hit. Like *I Dream of Jeannie* and *Gilligan's Island*, it wasn't well-received by early critics and certainly wasn't an industry favorite, but fans loved it. It maintained so much popularity through reruns that it enjoyed success in subsequent films, se-

Figure 4.2. (Left to right) Christopher Knight, Mike Lookinland, Eve Plumb, Ann B. Davis, Barry Williams, Maureen McCormick, and Susan Olsen in *The Brady Bunch*, Allstar Picture Library / Alamy Stock Photo

quels, and parodies. The show depicted the life of a large stepfamily, which is created when Mike Brady (Robert Reed), a father of three sons, marries Carol Martin (Florence Henderson), a mother of three girls. Their combined households result in oldest boy, Greg (Barry Williams), middle son, Peter (Christopher Knight), and youngest boy, Bobby (Mike Lookinland), oldest daughter, Marcia (Maureen McCormick), middle daughter, Jan (Eve Plumb), and youngest girl, Cindy (Susan Olsen). Like *Gilligan's Island*, Schwartz designed the series to address deeper issues, as each of the child characters represents various phases of the transition through childhood to adulthood.

The episode "Sergeant Emma,"[8] however, doesn't focus on the children necessarily; rather, it centers on their housekeeper, Alice Nelson (Ann B. Davis), and her cousin. Ann B. Davis plays both roles of Alice and her twin cousin, Emma, but this evil-twin depiction is admittedly different from others, maintaining connections in some areas while diverting in others. This very likely has something to do with the apparent goal of *The Brady Bunch* to focus primarily on issues of family and the wholesome experience. Thus, Emma, the evil twin depicted in *The Brady Bunch*, is devoid of all things sexual, versus other female evil twins, who are overtly sexual. It also has even more to do with the fact that a live-in housekeeper cannot function effectively if she is sexual or desirable, because she would serve as a threat to the woman of the house. For the other characters and the television audiences to accept Alice and Emma as grown women who "live" with and take care of a family of eight, they must appear asexual and undesirable, in order not to threaten the "other" woman, who is most often depicted as fragile, sexual, and desirable. Other than sexuality, though, Emma has a great deal in common with the other evil-twin depictions. Ultimately, this episode is used as a final example in my analysis because *The Brady Bunch* maintained such popularity with viewers that it became the premier example of a quintessential, tight-knit American family—twin-cousin housekeepers and all. In the following synopsis, I include what may be perceived as exhaustive details of the episode, but they are included in an effort to render clear the subsequent analysis.

The episode opens with Alice crossing the room to meet Carol and Mike, and she is wearing a bright yellow coat and carrying a bright red suitcase. Alice says, "I made out the shopping list, Mrs. Brady, and I just finished the wash and I don't think I've forgotten anything," but Carol interrupts her to tell her to stop worrying and to have a nice vacation. Alice assures them she will but then tears up, sobbing, "It broke my heart saying goodbye to the children. It's going to seem like a year since I'll see them again." Mike reminds Alice that she is only going to be gone a week, and Carol assures her that everyone will miss her too. Alice responds, "You know I wouldn't go if I didn't know you had a first-rate pinch hitter for me. You're gonna love my cousin Emma. She is efficient, well-organized, a born manager."

Then, we see Emma walking up the driveway. As with the other twins, her attire stands in stark contrast to Alice's. As mentioned, Alice is in a bright yellow coat, carrying a red suitcase, and Emma is wearing a dark green coat and deep red lipstick, walking militantly while carrying a dark-brown army-type duffle bag; additionally, Emma's natural hair color is depicted as black, mixed with gray, and Alice's hair is a lighter red color, also mixed with gray. As she approaches the house, Emma sees a bike on its side in the driveway and a football on the ground, so she picks up both, looking displeased. Alice notices her through the window and welcomes her in. Their mannerisms are as opposite as their looks: Alice is quick to smile and hug, whereas Emma is stoic and stiff. The Bradys meet Emma and tell her they hope she will feel welcome there; in a militant tone, Emma tells them the same. Alice leaves for her vacation, and Emma says to the Bradys, "I'm pretty sure I can handle the job, folks. I wasn't twenty years in the WAC [Women's Army Corps] for nothing. Most of that was as Master Sergeant." Carol and Mike are surprised to hear this and ask if her WAC job was difficult. Emma tells them that nothing is difficult, if one is organized. At that moment, we get the first real taste of how Emma will function as the evil twin to Alice's good twin. Two of the kids run into the house without closing the door, and in front of the parents, Emma shouts, "Halt! About face! Forward march and close the door! Hup two, hup two, move it along!" Then, she whispers to Mike and Carol, "It's just a question of *control.*"

The entire episode depicts the ways in which Emma takes control of the family. The next morning, she begins blowing the whistle and entering the bedrooms, wearing an Army uniform. She orders everyone to get up and start working, and when the boys resist, she responds, "Now, cut the chatter men. Suit up and fall out. Meet you in the yard in 15 minutes." She goes to the girls' room and shouts, "Rise and Shine girls. Breakfast is at 0800 hours." Everyone meets in the yard at six in the morning to exercise with Emma, who is now wearing a gray sweat suit, black shoes, and a whistle around her neck.

Figure 4.3.   Ann B. Davis as cousin Emma leads the Brady family on a jog in "Sergeant Emma," *The Brady Bunch*, Hulton Archive, Getty Images

The kids follow Emma's exercise instructions, but when they think they are finished, Emma shouts at them, "Never break formation without an order." Emma records their performance on a clipboard and then tells them to "fall out." Assuming they finally get to eat breakfast, the kids get excited. Emma blows the whistle, shouting, "Simmer down. There will be no chow until the inspection of quarters!"

In the next scene, the boys and girls are lined up side by side in the bedroom, where Emma inspects their shoes, drawers, beds, and cleanliness. She determines that their performance "will do" for the first time, and she dismisses them. Later, Carol expresses her concern over Emma to Mike, who says she is just a very organized person. Carol replies, "She's organized me right out of my own kitchen!" That evening, Emma conducts dinner just as she would a mess hall, which leaves Mike saying, "I feel like we've been drafted." For the remaining days of exercise, Mike and Carol are asked to join the kids, and Emma walks around with a yard stick, checking the form of each family member. During this scene, the episode loops the unofficial U.S. Army song "As Those Caissons Go Rolling Along" over their activities, as Emma takes and maintains more and more control over the family. Later, when Carol and Mike are relaxing in bed, Mike says, "If Emma weren't Alice's cousin, I'd ship her out for duty."

Carol and Mike decide they need to talk to Emma about these issues, so they find her in the kitchen "arranging the dishes in GI order." Emma asks, "Have you ever read the army manual on mess hall organization? You should. It's a real eye opener." Mike explains to Emma that they are concerned she has been working too hard and asks her if, even in the Army, she was given three-day passes for breaks. Emma replies, "Sure they did, but I never took them. Mr. and Mrs. Brady, I served 20 years in Uncle Sam's Army. I never goldbricked once, and I'm not about to start now. No sir, I've got a week here of special duty, and you're going to get every minute of it."

Since their plan to get Emma to take a break plan didn't work, the kids organize another plan. The kids borrow a small mouse from a friend and put it into the trash can, assuming Emma will be scared off upon finding it (because that trick always makes Alice scream). They yell for Emma, telling her there is a rat with huge fangs in the trash can. Unaffected, Emma walks over, picks up the mouse and says, "Oh, this little guy? Why he wouldn't hurt a fly. Remember, good soldiers aren't afraid of anything." Later, the other kids find Emma dusting while humming "As Those Caissons Go Rolling Along"; they try to convince Emma that she is coming down with an illness, but this plan also backfires, when Emma thinks it must have something to do with the daily exercise. She concludes, "I've been too easy on myself. I'm getting soft as a civilian." After all of their plans have failed, the episode provides a montage of Emma leading the family in exercises and showing them how to make a bed, fold a shirt, organize a closet, and roll a sock. Throughout this montage, all of the camera angles are canted, so as to express the disunity, disorientation, and discomfort of the situation.

The next day, Carol and Mike awaken to realize it is the day Alice returns and Emma leaves. Carol exclaims, "The prisoners of war are about to be liberated!" They decide to throw Alice a coming home party, so they order a party cake. Later, they are transferring the cake to a platter to prepare for Alice, when Emma walks in the kitchen. Carol tries to explain, but Emma says she understands: "It's my last day here and you want to give me a going-away party." The family embarrassingly concedes, and at the party, Emma tells them, "Well, troops, I never expected anything like this. I want you to know that this is the nicest thing that has happened to me, since I got the General Haggerty award for my campaign 'Make your barracks beautiful.' The army's a lonely life. I've loved every single minute I've been here."

Alice walks in the front door, and everyone hugs her. Alice says to Emma, "I guess you noticed that the Bradys are something special, and I guess you Bradys noticed that cousin Emma is something special, too." They answer, "She sure is special." Alice replies, "Now, I don't have to feel funny going away again. We can just ask cousin Emma to come back!" They all exchange concerned glances, and the episode ends.

"SERGEANT EMMA" ANALYSIS

First, this episode highlights an aspect of the series that seems inconsistent. Alice is depicted as loving the children so much that she cries at the idea of leaving them for a well-deserved, week-long vacation. Obviously, the series wants us to know that strong family-like bonds exist between Alice and the Bradys, yet Alice perpetually refers to Mike and Carol as the formal Mr. and Mrs. Brady, while they refer to her as Alice. If the series wanted viewers to assume the Bradys felt Alice was a part of the family, as she seems to feel she is, it is logical that she and Emma would be allowed and encouraged to call them by their first names. Regardless, the episode uses the light/dark trope to establish Alice and Emma as opposites from the beginning. Alice's bright clothes and lighter hair match her warm personality, and Emma's darker clothes and hair reflect her militant personality. When she is displeased by having to remedy normal occurrences for children, a bike on its side and a football on the ground, Emma's character, like the other evil twins, rejects domesticity and the nurturing aspects of motherhood. This is confirmed by her stiff greeting with the Bradys. She isn't portrayed as being flirtatious or conniving like other twins, but the depiction establishes her as the "other" to Alice's feminine norm. And Emma reveals by the end of the first scene what she believes is the most important quality of managing a family—having control.

Emma's disconnection from effective family management is further clarified, when she expects the family to adhere to her Army schedule. The more she uses military jargon and treats them as soldiers, the more we understand her placement in opposition of the "domestic goddess" trope. She is a different kind of evil but still evil. Thus, her loose inhibitions—her lack of self- control—involve her inability to "turn off" her militant lifestyle. Just as flirting makes Serena and Sister happy, even (or especially) when it isn't appropriate, commanding soldiers is Emma's catnip, even when it isn't appropriate. She upholds the military lifestyle even to the extent that she is comfortable depriving young kids of meals if they haven't dusted their rooms properly. In every aspect, she is incapable of being nurturing.

Emma's inability to function effectively in the domestic sphere has more to do with her career interests—her desire to function in the public sphere—than anything else. She defines her existence, not by her roles as wife, mother, or caretaker, but by her role as a Master Sergeant. The only way she can understand any role within the domestic sphere is to treat it the same way she treats her role in the public sphere. In discussing the television housewives of the fifties, in addition to the use of strong actresses to play docile characters, Leibman noticed that these types of characters performed their housework managerially, in the same way a career woman ran her office and that these depictions further convinced viewers that this type of housewife "was a career woman after all; it's just that her career was the home and family."⁹ Since Emma actually has a career outside of the home, though, unlike most housewife characters, even her strong, potentially valuable managerial skills are portrayed as anathema to domestic harmony.

Emma's intellectual prowess and political interests are intertwined with her strong career interests. She perpetually uses jargon and terminology that others do not understand, which greatly inhibits her ability to communicate. Her desire to use that jargon supersedes her desire to communicate, which again serves to impede her success in the role of a caretaker. When Emma rearranges the kitchen according to GI order and asks if the Bradys have read the manual, she is displaying a level of superiority. Even with adults, Emma claims to know what is best, thus establishing a parent-child relationship, even with Mike and Carol. This, again, is a by-product of Emma's need for control. Furthermore, she reiterates her devotion to Uncle Sam and the Army not only through mentions of awards and her mastery of certain manuals but also by humming the unofficial US Army song while she works. Her 20-year commitment to the military would easily and normally be regarded as admirable, but for the evil-split to be effective, Emma's career and dedication must be depicted as something that thwarts her ability to function normally in a society where females are expected to be masters of their private, domestic situations—not the military mess-hall settings of the public sphere. This is a good opportunity, though, to acknowledge how the show chooses to make Emma the master of mess-hall operations in the Army. Even within an evil-twin dynamic, where the characters are depicting an "us vs. them" mentality, Emma's primary function in the Army was in the kitchen and dining halls—the domestic areas of the military (although, in fairness, I suppose latrine duty would have been worse). This makes Emma's already socially unacceptable characterization, more acceptable.

Obviously, Emma is quintessential assertiveness. The entire episode centers on her asserting methods and authority over the Bradys. Even when she criticizes herself, she uses words like "I've become too soft" to describe her failures in character. As I've mentioned, in a telling montage sequence, Emma is instructing the household on how to do everything, from making beds to organizing closets, but every shot of the montage is filmed at an angle, so as to imply the unnatural, dysfunctional nature of Emma and the situation she has created within the domestic sphere. The canted angles also make the viewer feel generally uneasy about the scene and uncomfortable with a career Army professional attempting to run a household. Additionally, Emma's assertiveness is depicted as entrapment; just as Sister Jeannie is depicted as wanting to lock Tony in a cage and Serena turns Darrin into an ape, Emma's assertiveness has made the family, according to Carol, "prisoners of war." The Bradys do not warm to Emma until she displays some emotion at the pretend "going-away party," when she tells them that no one has ever done anything nice for her before. This scene bookends the episode; whereas Alice, the good cousin, begins the show by tearing up about leaving the children, Emma becomes more acceptable to them by tearing up upon leaving the family. But the episode doesn't leave viewers with the impression that Emma is anything like Alice—the split must be maintained. In that final scene, two things are emphasized. Both Alice and the family acknowledge how "special" Emma is, saying, "She sure is special, alright." And Emma reveals the ultimate result of being "special" in the sixties climate Friedan described. She admits in that final scene that she is lonely, just as the other evil twins are alone. Whether they claim to prefer it or not, they are all alone. The dominant message is clear: women who choose the private sphere enjoy the rewards of love and family, while those who choose the public sphere end up alone. And when the Bradys are thrilled with the return of Alice, the reaction parallels the social construction that America is pleased and running efficiently with the return of women from careers to the home.

This episode provides a nice transition to the non-American, *Doctor Who* example that follows. *The Brady Bunch*'s choice to depict Emma as functioning, not only in the public, career realm, but in the male-dominated realm of the 1960s military, is significant. This study began with dress-designing and babysitting careers for Patty and Cathy Lane, in *The Patty Duke Show*, but by the end of the decade, *The Brady Bunch* was depicting a woman as finding success in the male-dominated realm of the military, even though the by-product of that success is her inability to be perceived as a "normal" woman. Throughout the episode, Emma is aligned with masculinity, whether it is through the uniform she wears, the toughness and strength she exerts, the control she requires, or her supposed inability to nurture. She goes against "nature"; she is undesirable, prefers the "masculine" lifestyle of the military, and is in complete discord with the feminine realm of domesticity. Thus, her ways of communicating cannot be received effectively. Her alignment with masculinity, just like the other evil-twin alignments with sex, depict her as attempting to function in a space that was not designed for her, which leads to her inefficacy and loneliness. The underlying interpretation of loneliness is that an individual is unhappy, and in this way, the evil-twin depictions of the late sixties continue to embody Friedan's theory and further the feminine mystique.

DOCTOR WHO AND NON-AMERICAN TELEVISION
EXAMPLES OF FEMALE EVIL TWINS

Doctor Who is a science fiction show that began airing on the British Broadcasting Corporation (BBC) in 1963, a day after the assassination of John F. Kennedy. The show's premise involves the travels of "the doctor," an extraterrestrial who appears human, on his time-travel ship, the TARDIS. His assistant scientist is Liz Shaw. The original series ran from 1963 to 1989, becoming a cult-favorite in Britain, and in 2005, it enjoyed an enormously successful relaunch that made the show popular around the world. The long-running series has used different actors to play all of the roles throughout the series, including thirteen different actors for the doctor alone. The episode analyzed here, "Inferno,"[10] aired in the first part of 1970, in *Doctor Who*'s seventh season. It starred the third actor to portray the doctor, John Pertwee, and was the last episode to include Caroline John as scientist Liz Shaw. In this episode, the doctor travels sideways in time and encounters what he calls a "twin world." There, he finds identical counterparts for all of the key players in the show, including Shaw. This new world, however, is a fascist republic, and the inhabitants are attempting to drill to the center of the earth. As they drill closer, the core releases heat and poisonous gases, which threaten to transform humans into creatures and to potentially disintegrate the planet.

**Figure 4.4.   Jon Pertwee as the Doctor and Caroline John as Liz Shaw in *Doctor Who*,
RGR Collection / Alamy Stock Photo**

In this parallel world, Liz (whom I will refer to as Shaw in the parallel world) is a military officer instead of a scientist, which is why *The Brady Bunch* depiction of Emma transitions well to this episode. Both Emma and Shaw function in the public sphere in typically masculine roles, each displaying darker hair and dark military uniforms. But the significance of the BBC example is in how Shaw is depicted as being successful, while Emma is portrayed as incapable of operating normally. Shaw is multi-dimensional, while Emma and the other American good and evil twins are one-dimensional. The conclusion of this episode depicts Shaw very differently, while still maintaining her ties to and success in the public sphere.

"INFERNO" SYNOPSIS

When the doctor arrives in the twin world and sees a brunette in a military uniform who looks exactly like Liz, he asks, "Liz? Liz, it's me. Don't you recognize me? What's happened to everyone round here? Have you all gone mad? What are you doing in that ridiculous get-up?" Shaw (in the twin world) pulls a gun on him and tells him to put his hands up. The doctor still thinks it is the original Liz, so he tells her he can take a joke. She reminds him that she isn't joking, blows her whistle (also like Emma), and tells her assistant to take him away. The assistant responds, "Yes, Leader," and the doctor says she is being ridiculous. The doctor insists Shaw is the Liz he knows back "home," saying, "Now, wait. You are Elizabeth Shaw." Shaw responds, "I am Section Leader Elizabeth Shaw, yes." The doctor asks if she is a scientist, and she states that she is a military officer. The doctor's response serves to align the episode with American examples, when he notices the physical similarities and actual differences, saying, "Oh. This is fascinating. So many similarities, yet so many differences." Shaw tells her superior that she believes the doctor is a spy and that she has been on the phone with Central Records about the "prisoner." Central Records has no record of a person matching the doctor's description, so they conclude the situation is "like the doctor doesn't exist," but Shaw notes the strangeness of this because he appears to know so much about the drilling project, as if he had been a part of it for weeks.

The inhabitants of the twin world get very frustrated with the doctor not sharing who he "really is," and Shaw eventually threatens him: "Unless you co-operate, you'll soon be in front of a firing squad. You have very little time left." The doctor condescends, "My dear young lady, if that computer was functioning, it would warn us that we all have very little time left!" The assistant tells Shaw that he is going to take him out and shoot him, but Shaw insists that she will take charge of him. The doctor thanks her for saving his life, but she responds, "I am not concerned with saving your skin, only in carrying out the correct procedure." The doctor thanks her anyway and tells her that he may be able to repair their computer problem—a problem that is threatening the success of the mission. Shaw tells him it is not his concern, but as she is trying to escort him out, he quickly opens the panel on the back of the computer.

The assistant yells for him to proceed forward, but Shaw insists that they let him try. Even when the assistant resists a second time, Shaw says, "Let him try. We've got nothing to lose." The doctor quickly fixes the computer, just as the supervisor walks in and asks what is happening. Shaw says, "He has repaired the computer, Director," who chides her for allowing the prisoner to be anywhere near the computer in the first place. Shaw takes the doctor into the other room, where she asks him to tell her the truth, but he maintains that he is from a "parallel space-time continuum." She tells him there would be more hope for him if he told the truth, and the doctor describes the "twin world": "Your counterpart in the other world would tell you that I'm not in the habit of telling lies, Elizabeth." Shaw asks, "This other woman, the one that looks like me," and the doctor interrupts, "It's not that she looks like you, she *is* you. I do wish I could make you understand this." Shaw asks about her, and when the doctor tells her Liz is a scientist, Shaw reveals that she wanted to be a scientist too and even studied physics at the university. She finds that coincidental, but the doctor tells her that their minds run along similar parallels. The doctor pleads with her, "Look, Elizabeth, please try and think. Whatever they taught you in this bigoted world of yours, you've still got a mind of your own. Now use it, before it's too late!"

In an effort to appeal to Shaw's emotions, the doctor insists, "This other world exists. It's as true as the one you know yourselves." Shaw asks, "And we're all somehow duplicated there," and the doctor answers, "Yes. You, the Brigade Leader, Stahlman, Sutton, Petra, all of you. You could save your other selves." Shaw asks how they could save them, and the doctor explains the TARDIS to them. Another military officer asks, "So, we're expected to sacrifice all our lives so the doctor can get back to his other world," and Shaw answers, "We haven't got any lives to sacrifice. It's only a question of time." The Brigade Leader still doesn't believe the doctor, so Shaw insists, "You're outvoted, Brigade Leader. Let him go." They threaten to shoot the doctor, but Shaw distracts them, shouting, "Now's your chance, Doctor! Go on, Doctor! Go now!" Consequently, the twin world sacrifices their lives so that the parallel world may continue to exist.

"INFERNO" ANALYSIS

First, Shaw, the evil twin, sports the standard dark hair and dark clothes of other twins and (like Serena in *Bewitched*) exists in a darker world—a fascist republic. She also maintains strong career and political interests and displays exceptional intellectual prowess; Shaw is depicted as being supremely effective in her role in security, a profession that serves to protect the safety of others and is consequently usually dominated by males. The very nature of her career involves mastering the art of being assertive. Thus, this evil twin ticks almost all of the same boxes (minus loose inhibition) as the American versions, yet the overall interpretation is quite different. This analysis will examine the episode using the same established categories but will use them to reveal how the British treatment of this evil twin is different.

When we are first introduced to Shaw, she is asserting her authority in security by making orders of the doctor and commanding her assistant. She is referred to as "leader," so her character is immediately associated with governance and authority. In the first scene, she is also depicted as politically loyal and intelligent. She turns the doctor over to her superior and reveals her determination that the doctor could be serving as a spy. She has already been in contact with Central Records, which indicates she is not only smart, but quite proficient at her job. She and her good counterpart, Liz, are both depicted as functioning successfully and passionately in their public-sphere, masculine careers of security and science. They are different, but not oppositional.

At first, Shaw attempts to use power to control the doctor, but when that doesn't work, she is the only character open and willing to try alternatives. She deduces that they are going to die anyway if they do nothing, so she is the first to conclude that, even if the doctor has only a small chance of fixing their computer, it provides a higher chance of survival than their current situation. She uses logic, and she reasons with her male colleagues that the doctor should be allowed to try to fix the computer. The doctor's success in fixing the computer doesn't make her less effective in her security position, as she continues to tell him that there would be more hope for him if he would just tell them the truth. But it does make her more curious about his knowledge. She begins inquiring about this other world and her good counterpart, who is a scientist. The doctor is able to encourage Shaw to recall her own interest and success in science, as Shaw begins to see some parallels for herself—something that would require qualities of openness and humility that are not typical features of American career-woman depictions in the sixties.

Shaw appears to genuinely contemplate the doctor's explanation of a duplicate world that could be saved, and she asks questions and listens to the answers. Thus, she is depicted as logical, intelligent, and respected, without displaying the typical American evil-twin qualities of condescension, silliness, and impracticability. In fact, once Shaw realizes they can either save their counterparts or everyone can die, the episode presents another military officer asking, "So, we're expected to sacrifice all our lives, so the doctor can get back to his other world." Shaw displays the strongest ability in the room to reason intellectually, answering, "We haven't got any lives to sacrifice. It's only a question of time." When the Brigade Leader still doesn't believe the doctor, Shaw asserts herself successfully, insisting, "You're outvoted, Brigade Leader. Let him go." Having shown political loyalty thus far, Shaw chooses intellectual reasoning over political alliances when she decides to distract her colleagues and render them unable to shoot the doctor. She yells to the doctor, "Now's your chance, Doctor! Go on, Doctor! Go now!" Shaw is depicted as being supremely intellectual, career-minded, assertive, and politically loyal, but unlike American examples, these attributes do not function to cause her demise. Shaw succeeds in the public sphere. Furthermore, American depictions indicate a level of heartlessness in the evil-twin depictions. For example, Sister and Serena are often depicted as being so selfish that they do not notice or care about the needs of others. This *Doctor Who* example portrays twins who are both educated, trained, authoritative, and assertive; but those qualities don't preclude them from being compassionate. In the end, Shaw is the one to recognize that, if they are going to die anyway, it would be better for all of "humanity" if they could at least save the lives of an alternate universe. She allows herself to be open, flexible, humble, and malleable—all characteristics reserved solely for the good twins of American television. Consequently, Shaw comes across as possessing a level of wisdom that we aren't accustomed to seeing in evil-twin depictions. Ultimately, all of this means that, in American evil twins, the attributes of intellect, career interests, political interests, and assertiveness are represented and consumed as an indication that women associated with these attributes lack proper self-control, while the BBC *Doctor Who* example uses these qualities to reveal Shaw as having mastered, even ahead of her colleagues, the art of self-control in the process of difficult decision-making. Surprisingly, even though this episode appears to have been written and directed by men, the depiction shares the characteristics of the female-written American examples, which, like this example, depict the twins as being different but not oppositional.

NOTES

1. Sherwood Schwartz, *Inside Gilligan's Island: From Creation to Syndication* (Jefferson, NC: McFarland, 1988),167.

2. Cantor, *Gilligan Unbound*, 24.

3. Ibid., 16

4. Catherine Seipp, "Gilligan's Island vs the Taliban," in *Reason.com,* October 10, 2001, http://reason.com/archives/2001/10/10/gilligans-island-vs-the-taliba.

5. Ibid.

6. Schwartz, *Inside Gilligan's Island*, xv.

7. Cantor, *Gilligan Unbound*, 3.

8. *The Brady Bunch,* season 3, episode 20, "Sergeant Emma," written by Harry Winkler, directed by Jack Arnold, February 1972.

9. Leibman, *Living Room Lectures*, 193.

10. *Doctor Who*, season 7, episode 19, written by Don Houghton, directed by Douglas Camfield, May 1970.

5

Male Television Writers vs. Female Television Writers

The distinction of male versus female writing is especially important considering Friedan's realization that past images of the spirited girl were created by women and more contemporary images of the housewife-mother were created by men.[1] As I've mentioned, after WWII, as women were urged to leave the workforce and return to the home, women's magazine editors became largely male—men whose jobs were to identify and provide what female readers, largely housewives, would most like to encounter in these magazines. Friedan remembers a meeting with some of these male editors, as they described their assumptions of the needs of their female readers. One unnamed male editor said the following: "Our readers are housewives, full time. They're not interested in the broad public issues of the day. They are not interested in national or international affairs. They are only interested in the family and the home."[2] This is an important point because it highlights the differences between male and female engagement with Friedan's text and with visual cultures in general.

These series include episodes written by both men and women, sometimes as duos and sometimes independently. Of the 139 *I Dream of Jeannie* episodes, five were written or co-written by women, representing roughly 3.5 percent of the entire series, and of the 117 *Brady Bunch* episodes, 12 were written or co-written by women (10.3%). Unfortunately, none of the evil-twin episodes of either of those series was written or co-written by a woman, which makes a comparison of male and female perspectives difficult with *I Dream of Jeannie* and *The Brady Bunch. Bewitched, Gilligan's Island,* and *The Patty Duke Show,* however, provide different case studies. Of the 254 *Bewitched* episodes, 34 are written or co-written by women, representing about 13.38 percent of the series, and of the twenty-two evil-twin episodes, five are written or co-written by women, representing roughly 14.2 percent of those episodes. Of the 98 *Gilligan's Island* episodes, seven are written or co-written by women (7.14%), and the single evil-twin episode was written by a woman (100%). And for

The Patty Duke Show, three of the 104 episodes are co-written by women (2.88%). These three series make a comparison of gender perspectives possible, and considering all of these shows aired in the same decade, with many running concurrently and utilizing the same writers, it is also possible to compare female-written evil-twin episodes of *Bewitched, Gilligan's Island,* and *The Patty Duke Show* to male-written evil-twin episodes of *Jeannie* and *The Brady Bunch*. Incidentally, it is important to note that the fact that the two Sheldon vehicles, *Duke* and *Jeannie,* have drastically lower percentages of female writers shouldn't reflect anything about Sheldon's or the production teams' personal beliefs. Simply put, it wasn't that the shows weren't hiring any female writers; they just weren't hiring many writers in general because Sheldon wrote so many of the episodes himself.

When evil-twin episodes are written or co-written by women, the twins are presented less as an oppositional binary and more as a compatible, often symbiotic binary, where they are still depicted as opposites, but opposites who work together and, in some cases, need each other. Therefore, the female perspective reveals an image of the American woman that is both good and evil, self-serving and self-sacrificing, career-minded and homemaker. These female writers seem to indicate that the image of the American woman created by popular culture should be less of a strict oppositional binary, as male writers seemed to prefer, where women must fall into one side or the other of Friedan's split, and more of a complex combination of these qualities. And just as these female-written episodes depict good and evil twins who often rely on and need each other, they are implying the same balance exists within the American woman. Male writers seem to create twins with qualities that are so oppositional, they usually can't function effectively in each other's worlds. I argue that this has much to do with the male interpretation of Friedan's split, with the evil side—the career-minded, politically interested, assertive, self-serving woman—desiring power and control, rather than equality. Incidentally, this reflects a commonly held misnomer of feminism in general, that feminists want to control and have power over men instead of seeking equality. Male-written depictions of evil twins reflect the idea that women who fall on the evil side of the split desire control and power, reject domesticity, and consequently, serve as warnings. The evil twin almost always ends up alone. Thus, the warning conveyed to women through their depictions involves the idea that self-service and a rejection of domesticity will increase the potential of spinsterhood, while self-sacrifice guarantees companionship and security.

THE SPLIT FROM THE MALE PERSPECTIVE—POWER, CONTROL, AND A REJECTION OF DOMESTICITY

As mentioned, men wrote the vast majority of these evil-twin episodes, and the male-written episodes create stark boundaries in the split image; these writers depict the evil side as involving power, control, rejection of domesticity, and danger to men. In the *I Dream of Jeannie* episode, "Jeannie or the Tiger?" (written by James Henerson),

Sister is posing as Jeannie in an effort to steal Tony away from her. She begins trying to change Tony into what she wants him to be: a "swinging master in a white suit, smoking a cigar," she says. Jeannie, who obviously reflects the other side of the split image, says, "I like him just the way he is." In the end the two sisters have a "show-down" over Tony, where they use their magical abilities to hurl household objects at each other across the living room. Tony gets caught in the middle and is the only one injured. The message is clear: women with power want to control their men, and this is dangerous (literally) for the men involved.

In the *Jeannie* episode, "Ever Had a Jeannie Hate You?" (written by Sheldon under the pen name Allan Devon), Sister has prescribed Jeannie some love/hate potions and switched the bottles. Her motive is, again, to steal Tony away from Jeannie. Tony responds to her efforts: "I'm sorry lady but I've got work to do." He attempts to walk away, but Sister blinks him backwards to her, saying, "I can't wait to start training you. How you ever stood that square sister of mine, I'll never know. She and major Healy deserve each other." Tony asks Sister how she did it, and she says it was terribly easy . . . she switched the lotions. He says, "You're much smarter than Jeannie," and she replies, "Oh, I'm the greatest." Sister tells Tony that she is going to arrange for him to go 24 hours without sleep so that he can think of all the ways he is going to please her, and he responds by saying that he thought he was the master and she the genie. She says he is, but she runs a tight ship: "You'll see, you'll see." Tony asks if she minds if he drops by the office to grab a few things before he resigns. She says she doesn't know why he bothers but insists that he say, "pretty please" when he makes requests to her. He does and she says, "Alright, run along pet; but you better be back here by six o'clock . . . and don't be late because if I lose my temper, you'll just hate yourself." Tony goes to see Roger and Jeannie, who is under the spell of the switched love/hate potions, which means she loves Roger and hates Tony. Jeannie is mean to Tony, and Roger says, "Jeannie, control yourself." Tony tries to explain, claiming, "Your sister wants to make a slave out of me at six o'clock!"

Sister is depicted as needing power, control, and dominance. In the first scene, when Tony attempts to walk away, she forces him back and reminds him of how much she is looking forward to training him—she is in control. She also asserts herself as opposite of Jeannie by calling her sister "square." Then, when she is decid-ing what she wants to do with Tony, her actions are depicted as domineering. She demands that Tony speak in certain ways to her, saying "pretty please," for example. She wants Tony to think about all of the ways he can please her, like a master/slave relationship. When the scene depicts Jeannie, who is under the spell of Sister's lo-tions, Roger tells her to "control herself." Last, when Tony explains his situation to Roger and Jeannie, he refers to the master/slave relationship again, saying, "Your sister wants to make a slave of me." In all of these male-written scenes, Sister is de-picted as selfish, controlling, and power-hungry, while Jeannie is reminded by Roger that she needs to be self-controlled.

In the end of most "evil-twin" episodes of *I Dream of Jeannie*, Sister is contained in some capacity. For example, in the episode "Tony's Wife"[3] (written by Sheldon as

Christopher Golato), Tony traps Sister in a perfume bottle at the end of the episode, saying to Jeannie, "You are going to put her some place where we don't have to worry about her . . . where we won't have to think about her for two thousand years." Tony might as well have been speaking of "the problem that has no name"—the voice housewives suppress—or the voice of feminism. Sister Jeannie represents that voice, and Tony wants Jeannie to put it some place where they never have to worry about it again.

In the episode "Genie, Genie, Who's Got the Genie?, Part 3"[4] (written by James Henerson), Sister traps Tony and Roger in cages, while a harem of females gaze at them, thereby subverting the male gaze. Tony tries to infantilize Sister, saying, "Now, you look here, young lady." She doesn't like this treatment, so she responds by treating him like a child, telling him if he is good, she might let him out for some exercise. Sister is depicted as a powerful woman, who wants to use those powers exclusively to control men. In another episode, "How to Marry an Astronaut"[5] (written by James Henerson), Sister tries to give Jeannie a crash course on getting a man to marry her, saying, "Sis, wake up, no man gets married of his own free will. They have to be led, persuaded, cajoled. You just have to know the tricks." All of these *Jeannie* examples highlight the male perspective that feminism, represented by Sister, means women seek dominance and power over men, rather than merely equality.

Bewitched applies a similar treatment in the male-written episodes. In the first evil-twin episode of the series, "And Then There Were Three,"[6] when Serena and Darrin disagree about something, she puts him in a Native American costume—a costume that renders him as a savage—and binds and gags him. In the episode "Double, Double, Toil and Trouble,"[7] when Serena poses as Samantha, and Darrin tells her to come over and give him a kiss, she responds, "If you want a kiss, come and get it." Both examples depict Serena as powerful and controlling. Furthermore, in the episode "Hippie, Hippie, Hooray,"[8] Darrin is explaining to Larry how different Samantha and Serena are, saying, "Sam is Sam and Serena is Serena, and Sam couldn't be Serena if she tried." Later, Darrin is bragging to a client about Sam's wonderful domestic abilities, but when Serena shows up posing as Sam, she is dressed like a "hippie" and immediately kisses Darrin passionately, which forces the client to ask, "This is a girl who bakes her own bread?" Both examples reflect the idea that woman can either be one or the other; she can't have qualities of both sides of the split. Furthermore, the evil twins are, in the end, depicted as dissatisfied and unhappy individuals, while Samantha and Jeannie are portrayed as content. This is the ultimate male-written message regarding the split: give up the fun and retain the happiness. A woman cannot have both.

In "Serena's Youth Pill" (written by Michael Morris), Samantha uses foreign languages to summon her cousin (tapping into Serena's own intellectual prowess), saying, "In gay Paris, it's 's'il vous plait,' in Germany, it's bitte. Please, Serena, come this way. I need a baby-sitter." Serena appears and responds, "Ha! Do I look like Mary Poppins to you?" Samantha says, "Well, I'll admit, it's casting against type. But Esmeralda's not available, and I have a charity luncheon to go to." In order to communicate with Serena, Samantha must use intellect—the ability to speak multiple languages. When Serena ascertains why she has been summoned, she places herself in opposition to a quintessential domestic Goddess, Mary Poppins, and Samantha admits that Serena does not normally possess these capabilities.

In another example, Larry has unknowingly just seen Serena; assuming she is Samantha, he fears Samantha is on the verge of becoming a hippie—a part of the counterculture. Larry says to Darrin, "Forget about the account. It's you I care about and that poor little girl Samantha." To convince Larry that Samantha is not becoming a hippie, Darrin invites Larry and Louise to dinner. He wants them to see Samantha and Serena together, so they can understand them as separate people, but Serena will not show up. Darrin tells Samantha that Serena isn't appearing, and Samantha believes that she can portray both Samantha and Serena for the evening, when they aren't in the room together. Then she notes, "Except that, I can't be both of us at the same time." This episode serves to align Serena with the counterculture, and then have Samantha express explicitly that a woman cannot be both sides of the split at the same time—she can either be one or the other.

These male-written episodes also involve the evil twins rejecting domesticity, as they are almost always either incapable of or unwilling to perform domestic duties. In *I Dream of Jeannie*, Sister makes Jeannie's fresh-out-of-the-oven cake fall flat when she wants to irritate her. In *Bewitched*, Serena is often asked to babysit, but she rarely performs this job appropriately, as she makes storybook characters come to life and magically produces an actual milk cow when the children want glasses of milk with lunch. Whenever Samantha is working in the kitchen, Serena will not help her; she will only eat the food being prepared. When Serena tries to work an electric mixer in the kitchen, for example, she bumbles it and fails miserably. In this way, the male-written episodes depict the evil twins as being incapable of functioning within the domestic sphere, thus adopting qualities of the opposite sex, which television deems, according to Leibman, as being an indicator of evil in women.

In "Marriage, Witch's Style" (written by Michael Morris), Samantha has baked a cake and is icing it, while she sings a jingle about cake batter. Magically, a slice is removed from the cake, and Samantha asks, "Okay, who's the wise witch?" It is worth noting how often Samantha refers to Serena as "wise" (even if she is being sarcastic), thus reinforcing Serena's intellectual prowess. Serena appears in a long fur tiger coat (always the hunter), saying, "Hi, little cousin. You made it sound so yummy." Samantha insists, "Put that piece of cake back," and Serena responds, "You can have your piece of cake back. Calories kill the figure." Samantha is aligned with domesticity and happiness (the singing), while Serena is depicted as the hunter (fur coat) and self-obsessed (concerned with figure). In a similar example, "Chance on Love" (written by John L. Green), Samantha arrives home with a bag full of groceries. The items magically begin to be placed in cabinets. Again, Samantha asks, "Okay, who's the wise witch?" Serena answers, "Wiser than you are cousin, drudging around the kitchen like a slave." Samantha reminds her that "doing housework is one of the joys of living the mortal life. It means you are doing something for someone you love." Serena attempts to change Sam's mind, saying, "Instead, why don't you break out and join me and the maharaja Manipur. He's throwing an elephant race." Furthermore, in "The Corsican Cousins" (written by Ed Jurist), Endora attempts to persuade Samantha to be more like Serena. Serena is dancing on TV, so Endora says to Sam, "Why don't you take some advice from your cousin Serena. She is quicksilver. She lives in the sparkle of a star and a flash of color. See all the fun you're missing?" Samantha replies, "I wouldn't trade Darrin for a hundred of them." In all of these examples, Serena functions explicitly to thwart Samantha's domestic abilities, whether that means slicing a cake or mixing up groceries. Each time, Serena and Endora try to convince Samantha of the "fun" the "other side" has, while Samantha perpetually expresses her satisfaction and fulfillment in a life of service. These male-written episodes serve to establish and perpetuate the complete opposition of good and evil twins.

THE SPLIT FROM THE FEMALE PERSPECTIVE —DIFFERENT *AND* COMPATIBLE

Episodes written or co-written by women depict a very different type of evil twin. In these episodes, the good and evil twins are depicted as inhabiting qualities of both sides of the split, good and evil, and they use these qualities to work together. For example, the *Bewitched* episode "Samantha's Power Failure," co-written by Lila Garrett, serves as a significant example of the differences between male-written and female-written episodes. Samantha has been stripped of her powers for not appearing before the Witches Council—something she missed for family reasons. Surprisingly, though, Serena and Uncle Arthur support Samantha's stance. In the first scene, Serena appears in the living room in a white karate uniform (discussed earlier as career interests). She has just chopped the coffee table into two pieces and tells Sam that she won her platinum belt. Sam asks, "Do you have to practice on my furniture?" In male-writtten depictions, Serena almost never apologizes for anything, but here, she says, "Oh, sorry about that. I'll fix it. I can't stay long, little Cuz. I have to split to India for the world rope climbing championship." Endora interrupts, saying, "Alright, alright, will the shepherd (Uncle Arthur) take the black sheep (Serena) and go rope climbing! Samantha and I are having a serious conversation." Uncle Arthur reveals that their purpose in being there is to support Samantha. Serena responds, "Don't worry, little cousin, we are behind you 100%," and Uncle Arthur says, "Don't let the council split you and Darrin." The inclusion of this statement is especially important, considering that in most episodes, Samantha's family members are perpetually trying to wreak havoc on her relationship with Darrin, but here, they have arrived to preserve it. Serena even says the following about Samantha and Darrin: "No, you're a set . . . sorta mismatched, but a set. As we were saying, little cousin, you just hang in there. You can count on us." Uncle Arthur confirms this, saying, "No matter what. We're at your side. Sammy, the ship may be sinking, but we'll stick by you, even if we all go down together . . . come on, Serena, let's pledge our loyalty." Uncle Arthur and Serena are so committed to remaining loyal to Samantha that the council also strips them of their powers. Incidentally, Serena's ever-changing birth mark is a peace sign in this episode, which happens to reflect her atypical pursuits to maintain peace in the family.

Later in the episode, Samantha, Serena, and Uncle Arthur are in the kitchen together. Serena apologetically says to Samantha, "Face it. We're drags. We should all cut out of your life completely." Sam replies, "Nonsense, the only reason you were cut in is because of me." Both twins are taking the blame and apologizing to each other. This solidarity inspires Samantha to assert herself in front of the Witches Council, by using the following logic: "Do you remember the Salem witch trials, when women were killed just for being different? Remember how angry you were at that injustice? This is no different. You are condemning me just because I am different, but even if you take away my powers, I will still be a witch."

This episode, the lead writer of which is a woman, includes very different twin representations. First, Samantha is the one who is presented as being defective—she has lost her powers. Serena arrives, not to make matters worse, but to express her loyalty to Sam, her willingness to work with her as a team. She even expresses her insistence that Samantha remain dependent on Darrin—something she absolutely resists in male-written episodes. Serena makes her commitment to Samantha explicit ("I'm behind you 100%"), and when this results in her own loss of power, she represents the sacrifice and service that is typical of the good side of the split. She takes this even further by insisting to Samantha that she belongs with Darrin, that they are a pair. Serena is depicted as not only working to support Samantha, but as embodying the elements of service we do not normally see in evil twins. In the final scene, when Samantha feels badly that her situation has negatively affected the others, Serena admits that she feels she should "cut out" of Samantha's life completely to make it better. This sacrificial statement inspires Samantha to be assertive, as she chooses to appear in front of the council and expose their unfairness. Samantha employs assertiveness in her tone and intellectual prowess in her use of historical allegory—two traits that always fall on the evil side of the split in male-written episodes. At the same time, Serena employs understanding, supportiveness, and a desire for solidarity—all attributes rarely embodied by evil twins. Both twins have taken on attributes of the other side, and in the end, unlike male-written episodes, the twins are successful in both spheres.

In the episode, "It's So Nice to Have a Spouse Around the House," written by Barbara Avedon, the opening scene presents Sam's apron being magically removed from her. This is Sam's clue that Endora is present. She has arrived to tell Samantha that she is again needed to serve at the head of the Witches Council. This means Samantha must leave Darrin temporarily, but Darrin responds selfishly, "Let's get something straight. First, you're a wife. Then, you're a witch. A wife's place is with her husband." Sam responds with uncharacteristic sarcasm, asking, "Good, then I get to play golf with you this afternoon?" In an effort to compromise, Sam asks Serena to fill in for her as housewife, while she appears before the council. Serena agrees to help. In this female-written episode, not only does Samantha make an atypical point about male/female inequality—good women spend weekends cleaning house, while good husbands play golf—but also, she and her evil twin work together to find a solution to Samantha's need to be away from the home. Through Darrin, the episode conveys the message that popular culture regards Darrin's self-service activities, including golf, as acceptable behavior for husbands, and Samantha's self-service activities, including appearing before the council, as unacceptable activities for good wives. Together, the cousins, good and evil, work to identify these inequities, and to establish ways—albeit ways that require two females, while televised male self-service requires no accommodation at all—for Samantha to engage in necessary forms of self-service.

Similarly, in the episode "Mrs. Stephens, Where Are You?," co-written by Peggy Chantler Dick, Sam calls Serena to babysit for her while she leaves the house to ship a package to Darrin. Incidentally, Serena's beauty mark, which changes every episode and typically reflects the content of the episode, is the Ankh in this episode—the Egyptian symbol for life and magical protection. Serena serves as the children's protection throughout the episode, self-sacrificing for Sam while she runs an errand. In this way, the characters adopt each other's traits, as Serena succeeds in the private sphere while Samantha ventures out into the public sphere. And, in the episode "Samantha and the Troll," co-written by Lila Garrett, Serena appears in the kitchen and notices Samantha is not well. Serena happily offers to watch the kids while Samantha sees a doctor. Again, these cousins work together to solve the problem, even though they are still depicted as different from each other. Female writers create characters who are compatible, even while different, by portraying cousins, good and evil, working together.

In another female-written episode, Samantha talks to Tabitha about equal rights for women. In "Tabitha's Very Own Samantha," written by Shirley Gordon, Samantha says to Tabitha, "Real life mommies sometimes have to say 'no,' but they still love you." Then later to Darrin, she says she wants Tabitha to know "the women around here still have equal rights . . ." And, finally, in the episode "Darrin Goes Ape," co-written by Pauline Townsend, Serena brings Darrin a gift, one she means sincerely. But Darrin rejects the gift because it involves magic, and Serena is offended. Samantha disagrees with Darrin's reaction, and Darrin admits, "I'm not really mad at Serena, actually. How could I be that mad when I love her cousin so much?" In this female co-written episode, the show acknowledges that women inhabit qualities from both sides of the split. By marrying Samantha, Darrin not only gets her, he gets the evil cousin too. Just as women in reality embody qualities of both sides of the split, Darrin must be accepting of Serena (woman's evil side), if he is to get to love Samantha (woman's good side).

The Patty Duke Show and *Gilligan's Island* also present episodes where good and evil twins work together when episodes are written or co-written by women. In *The Patty Duke Show* episode, "Slumber Party," co-written by Pauline Townsend, who also contributed to *Bewitched* evil-twin episodes, Ross is caught recording the girls' conversations at a slumber party. Patty and Cathy team up and work together to get back at Ross. This episode does not contain the standard dynamic where Patty wants to get back at Ross and Cathy wants to be prudent. Both cousins are in agreement in their mission to teach a lesson to Ross; consequently, they work together as equals throughout the episode. In the end, this results in the girls telling Ross they love him, and he repeats it back to them. Similarly, in the *Gilligan's Island* episode, "All About Eva," written by Joanna Lee, we witness castaway women, Ginger and Mary Ann, who are willing to look past their differences with Eva, in an effort to perform a teamwork makeover and improve Eva's quality of life back home. The episode doesn't end with the same warm feelings expressed in these scenes, but it does depict opposite women working together—as a team—toward the good and happiness of other women.

In this way, the female writers of *Bewitched*, *The Patty Duke Show*, and *Gilligan's Island* make a compelling response to Friedan's text, one that acknowledges and underscores the many complexities of women—the image of which cannot in reality be so easily split into two oppositional binaries. In performing this research in the years of 2017–2019, I couldn't help but notice the ways in which the current popular Amazon series, *The Marvelous Mrs. Maisel*, maintained these practices established in the 1960s. The series is set in 1958 Manhattan, and in the first season, Miriam "Midge" Maisel (Rachel Brosnahan) does whatever she can to help her husband, Joel (Michael Zegen), achieve his dream of being a stand-up comedian. In a scene that connects private with public spheres and domesticity with career, she makes a brisket to bribe club managers to give Joel good time slots for his routines. She also records audience responses to jokes and takes notes on potential content for future gigs. One night, when Joel leaves her to have a relationship with his secretary, Midge gets drunk, heads to the club herself, and brings down the house with her improvised stand-up routine about her life as a 1950s housewife. In the entire first season, viewers get to enjoy watching her juggle these roles as homemaker, mother, daughter, divorcee, and stand-up female comedian in the 1950s. Initially, I was excited to connect my research on the evil twins of 1960s television with Midge, who, in the first season, seems to embody both sides of the split in one person—a person portrayed in the 1950s yet witnessed in the twenty-first century. However, the second season of *The Marvelous Mrs. Maisel* only served to prove that the 1960s representations of women still persist today. In the second season, Midge has two jobs, one at a department store and the other as a comedian with a manager (Alex Bronstein). But unlike the first season, we don't see Midge perform any tasks of maternal practice. In fact, her children are almost completely absent throughout the entire second season, leaving us to wonder where they are and who is caring for them. As Midge assumes her new career as a stand-up comedian, she relinquishes the maternal duties we witnessed in the first season—duties that made the show so interesting; in the second season, she has transitioned from a character that embodies both sides of the split to one that depicts only the qualities of the evil side. We never see her cook, clean, or care for the children in the entire second season, and even during her month-long vacation to the Catskills, the children are completely absent from her daily life. In other words, her desire to have a successful career is depicted as causing her to forget about and lose interest in her role as a mother—something with which the average parent viewer, whether viewing in the sixties or in the twenty-first century, likely can't identify. Consequently, the final episode of the series is quite possibly the most revealing piece of evidence regarding the power and persistence of the split-woman image, as it is titled "All Alone." That's exactly how Midge's careerist choices have left her: all alone. This example connects Friedan's observations in 1963 with current period pieces of the decade. To conclude with the 1960s examples, though, even though the female writers make strides regarding popular culture's image of the American women, by depicting Jeannie, Samantha, and Cathy as utterly fulfilled in their service, and their twins as perpetually restless and dissatisfied, the evil twins, like Midge Maisel, are left to serve as warnings: indulge that evil voice, and one might end up unhappy and alone.

NOTES

1. Friedan, *The Feminine Mystique*, 54.

2. Ibid., 37.

3. *I Dream of Jeannie*, season 3, episode 11, "Tony's Wife," written by Christopher Golato, directed by Claudio Guzman, November 1967.

4. *I Dream of Jeannie*, season 3, episode 18, "Genie, Genie, Who's Got the Genie?, Part 3," written by James Henerson, directed by Hal Cooper, January 1968.

5. *I Dream of Jeannie*, season 4, episode 10, "How to Marry an Astronaut," written by James Henerson, directed by Hal Cooper, December 1968.

6. *Bewitched*, season 2, episode 18, "And Then There Were Three," written by Bernard Slade, directed by William Asher, January 1966.

7. *Bewitched*, season 4, episode 4, "Double, Double, Toil and Trouble," written by Ed Jurist, directed by William Asher, September 1967.

8. *Bewitched*, season 4, episode 21, "Hippie, Hippie, Hooray," written by Michael Morris, directed by William Asher, February 1968.

Conclusion

I have often been asked why I continue to spend so much time researching television series that began airing over fifty years ago. Thus far, my responses have always involved something about how I grew up watching these shows and how they served to program my own observations and experiences as an adult, student, teacher, and scholar. This study, however, reveals that these shows seem to have had more of a profound impact on American television tropes, in general, than I anticipated. In particular, the differences I observe regarding female evil-twin depictions and male evil-twin depictions continue to persist today: even in more recent series, male evil twins either continue to embody actual evil (e.g., murder) or find themselves astonished by their similarities, while female evil twins embody evils that are less like crime and more like the typical flaws of humanity (e.g., jealousy and greed).

After the sixties and seventies, popular shows such as *Knight Rider* (1980s), *Friends* (1990s), and *Sabrina the Teenage Witch* (2000s) continued to use the twinning trope, but the patterns established in the sixties persist. For example, in the "Goliath"[1] episodes of *Knight Rider*, Michael Knight (David Hasselhoff) meets his evil twin Garth (also played by David Hasselhoff), who has a dark goatee, mustache, and sideburns, wears a white suit and diamond jewelry, and carries a cane. When Michael asks a female casino worker about Garth, she says, "Do you know what antithesis means? You are the antithesis of Garth. I've never seen two people who look so much alike and who are so different inside." Garth has spent the past several years in prison but has returned in an effort to steal KITT's (Michael's interactive car) molecular formula. Garth's ultimate goal, though, is to kill Michael, saying, "Mark my words; Michael Knight will die." As with the sixties examples of *Bonanza* and *Star Trek*, Garth is an evil twin who desires actual evil—theft and murder.

In the *Sabrina the Teenage Witch* (1996–2003) episode "The Good, The Bad, and The Luau,"[2] Sabrina Spellman (Melissa Joan Hart) finds out that every Spellman is born with a twin. She and her family travel to Maui to meet the twin, which is standard practice in their familial history. Sabrina meets Katrina (also played by Melissa Joan Hart), and they spend the first few days getting along as best friends. Then, both girls are told they must go in front of the Witches Tribune to determine which twin will be deemed the good twin and which twin will be the evil twin, because for each set of twins, there must be one and the other, this and that. Both girls answer a series of questions, while the presiding judge makes his decision. They are asked to provide examples of their goodness. Sabrina claims that she recently used her magic to help a pregnant cat, but Sabrina's cat Salem reminds her that she actually only helped the pregnant cat because Salem promised to help her solve a puzzle. Sabrina says, "You're right; I was selfish, and being selfish is a Spellman's worst trait. I'm evil and doomed." The judge appears to agree with Sabrina's assessment of herself and decides she *is* the evil twin, and her punishment is to be shoved into the lava of a volcano, which is the only way to strip a witch of her powers (the witch will not be killed by the lava). Once Sabrina and Katrina arrive at the top of the volcano, the judge tells Katrina to push Sabrina into the volcano. She does, but Sabrina catches a branch on her way down. The judge reveals that this was the final test—only an evil twin is actually able to push another witch into a volcano, so Katrina must be the evil twin. In later episodes,[3] Katrina's evil includes telling Sabrina she looks like she has gained weight and taking Sabrina's passport from her. In other words, Katrina's evil is very different from Garth's evil in *Knight Rider*; still, these details are consistent with the patterns established by the twins of sixties television. Since this *Sabrina* episode references Friedan's split so explicitly (i.e., the dialogue even states that when dealing with twins, one must be good and one must be evil) and strongly highlights connections of selfishness and evil in women, it is worth noting that the episode was both directed and written by women (Linda Day and Nancy Cohen, respectively). It seems plausible that these female writers were attempting to comment directly on the firmly established patterns of the television twinning trope and the trope's relationships with Friedan.

Of all of these contemporary examples, the series *Friends* (1994–2004) is easily the most popular series addressed here. It is significant to this study because, other than *Gilligan's Island*, it is one of the only series to include both male and female twins, Phoebe Buffay's evil sister Ursula Buffay (both parts played by Lisa Kudrow) and Ross Geller's twin Russ (both roles played by David Schwimmer). I end with this television example because it connects well with my first example, *The Patty Duke Show*, and maintains the same patterns established 40 years prior. In the episode "The One with Two Parts, Part 1 and 2,"[4] we are introduced to Ursula, Phoebe's evil twin sister. Joey (Matt LeBlanc) and Chandler (Matthew Perry) are dining at a restaurant, when they see Ursula (thinking it is Phoebe) waiting on tables. On the way home, Chandler discusses how similar Phoebe and Ursula appear, but Joey establishes their differences immediately, saying "Phoebe is Phoebe, and Ursula is . . . well . . . hot . . . She's different." As he often does, Joey decides he wants to pursue Ursula romantically. Later, the friends, Rachel (Jennifer Aniston), Monica (Courtney Cox), Ross, Chandler, and

Phoebe are in the living room watching *The Patty Duke Show* on television. Seeing the televised twins reminds Phoebe of Ursula, and she demands they turn off the show. They ask her what's wrong with Joey dating Ursula, and Phoebe describes how mean Ursula has been to her throughout her life, stealing her boyfriends and smashing her property (again, not real evil, but television's version of "female evil"). Phoebe eventually decides to discuss the Ursula situation with Joey, but when she knocks on his door, Ursula answers it, wearing nothing but one of Joey's shirts, thus maintaining the sexual excess trends established by previous female evil twins.

Friends provides a very different treatment for the twins Ross and Russ. Rather than highlight their differences, the episode focuses on their similarities. In other words, with these male evil twins, the trope does not demand that one be good and one be evil. In the episode "The One with Russ," [5] Rachel decides to begin dating again, following her breakup with Ross. However, her new date, Russ, looks and acts exactly like Ross. The friends spend most of the episode trying to get Rachel to see their similarities. In fact, whereas in *Bewitched* Darrin says "Samantha is Samantha and Serena is Serena," in *Gilligan's Island*, Ginger tells Mary Ann that Eva could never be Ginger Grant because "there is only one Ginger Grant," and in *Friends*, Joey says in the aforementioned episode, "Phoebe is Phoebe, and Ursula is . . . well . . . hot," in this episode, Phoebe says of Ross and Russ, "Ross is Russ, and Russ is Ross"—a statement that stands in clear opposition to descriptions of the female evil twins. The sixties message of oppositional/binary roles for women and more synthesized/holistic roles for men remains the same, even into the 21st century.

As a final example of the persistence of these images, the 2018 film *Venom*,[6] based on the Marvel Comics character, follows the story of Eddie Brock (Tom Hardy), a journalist investigating a scandal that involves people dying during "medical" test trials. To demonstrate the film's popularity, in addition to achieving recognition because of its relationship with the Marvel franchise, the film maintained 81% in audience popularity on *RottenTomatoes.com*; thus, it is a film that has been viewed and enjoyed by many. During Eddie's investigation, an alien symbiote chooses Eddie as a host; thus, Eddie inherits the violent super alter ego Venom. Prior to finding Eddie, the alien had attempted to combine with three separate female individuals, but each female host becomes murderous, rather than strengthened by the symbiote. It is interesting that Marvel actually uses the term symbiote for the alien, because it means the relationship between alter ego and host will be mutually beneficial to each other. Yet, when the symbiote attempts to combine with women, a mutually beneficial relationship proves to be impossible. The alter ego's relationship with Eddie is very different. Like the female characters, the alien and Eddie are two very different entities, each having different voices (even though both characters are played by Tom Hardy), needs, strengths, and weaknesses, but unlike the female hosts, Eddie and the symbiote are able to work together for mutual benefit. Eddie provides the alter ego with food and a "vehicle," and the symbiote provides Eddie with power and protection. When the alter ego first reveals half of his face to Eddie, Eddie asks, "What the hell are you?" The alter ego responds, "*We* are Venom . . . It is *we*; it is going to take *both* of us." Later, the alter ego acknowledges, "I'm starting to like you. You and I are not so different." By the end of the movie, the symbiotic pair decide their union can be permanent. Eddie/Venom asks himself, "What do you want to do tonight?" Eddie/Venom responds to himself, "The way I see it, *we* can do whatever we want." Each time the word "we" is used, it is emphasized. Ultimately, this film provides another example of a male evil alter ego that is actually evil, one that even comes with a name that literally means poison, but the alter ego functions as poison only with female hosts. As with the *Bonanza* and *Star Trek* examples, male alter egos are depicted as being actual evil. Venom's potential damage to humanity goes far beyond intellectual prowess and career interests, as we witness with female alter egos. But even considering the evil of Venom, Eddie is able to embody both of them—good and evil. In fact, Eddie is able to program the two sides of his "person" not only to get along with each other but also to benefit from the strengths of the other. Thus, even presently, the image of woman still conveys the message that success can be found only in choosing the good side of a "this or that" society, while male depictions maintain much more flexibility.

I conclude with the example of *Venom* because it exemplifies in a contemporary context so many of my favorite quotes from this study. Friedan claimed that women in reality embody the split; Moya Luckett regarded the female twinning trope as a disruption of identity; the film *The Dark Mirror* put forth the idea that twins function to mirror each other—"everything in reverse"; and Patty Duke admitted that her characters on the show could not be two whole people—in order to create one, she would have to take from the other. All of these statements underscore the binary aspects of the twinning trope when dealing with female characters, while male alter-ego examples, such as Russ/Ross in *Friends* and Eddie/Venom in *Venom* have become increasingly synthesized, focusing more on similarities than on oppositions. Ultimately, these details serve to underscore the significance of 1960s television in the construction of American popular culture identities, the persistence and impact of prominent trends in the visual cultures of any decade, and the importance of recognizing meaning in the images that shape our daily realities.

NOTES

1. *Knight Rider*, season 2, episode 1, "Goliath," written by Glen A. Larson, directed by Winrich Kolbe, October 1983.

2. *Sabrina, The Teenage Witch*, season 3, episode 25, "The Good, the Bad and the Luau," written by Jonathon Schmock and Nancy Cohen, directed by Linda Day, May 1999.

3. These episodes include "You Can't Twin" (2000) and "Deliver Us from E-mail" (2002).

4. *Friends*, season 1, episode 16, "The One with Two Parts," written by Marta Kauffman and David Crane, directed by Michael Lembeck, February 1995.

5. *Friends*, season 2, episode 10, "The One with Russ," written by Ira Ungerleider, directed by Thomas Schlamme, January 1996.

6. *Venom*, written by Jeff Pinker (screenplay and story), Scott Rosenberg (screenplay and story), and Kelly Marcel (screenplay), directed by Ruben Fleischer, 2018.

Bibliography

Attallah, Paul. "The Unworthy Discourse: Situation Comedy in Television." *Critiquing the Sitcom*. Ed. Joanne Morreale. (Syracuse, NY: Syracuse UP, 2003), 91-115.

Bell, Book, and Candle. Written by Daniel Taradash (screenplay) and John Van Druten (play). Directed by Richard Quine. Julien Blaustein Productions, December 1958.

Bewitched. Season 2, episode 18. "And Then There Were Three." Written by Bernard Slade. Directed by William Asher. Sony Pictures, January 1966.

Bewitched. Season 2, episode 21. "Fastest Gun on Madison Avenue." Written by Lee Erwin. Directed by William Asher. Sony Pictures, February 1966.

Bewitched. Season 4, episode 4. "Double, Double, Toil and Trouble." Written by Ed Jurist. Directed by William Asher. Sony Pictures, September 1967.

Bewitched. Season 4, episode 19. "Snob in the Grass." Written by Ed Jurist. Directed by R. Robert Rosenbaum. Sony Pictures, January 1968.

Bewitched. Season 5, episode 2. "Samantha Goes South for a Spell." Written by Ed Jurist. Directed by William Asher. Sony Pictures, October 1968.

Bewitched. Season 5, episode 5. "It's So Nice to Have a Spouse Around the House." Written by Barbara Avedon. Directed by William Asher. Sony Pictures, October 1968.

Bewitched. Season 5, episode 16. "Cousin Serena Strikes Again, Part 2." Written by Ed Jurist. Directed by Richard Michaels. Sony Pictures, January 1969.

Bewitched. Season 5, episode 20. "Mrs. Stephens, Where Are You." Written by Peggy Chantler Dick and Douglas Dick. Directed by Richard Michaels. Sony Pictures, February 1969.

Bewitched. Season 5, episode 21. "Marriage, Witches' Style." Written by Michael Morris. Directed by William Asher. Sony Pictures, February 1969.

Bewitched. Season 5, episode 25. "Samantha's Power Failure." Written by Lila Garrett and Bernie Kahn. Directed by William Asher. Sony Pictures, March 1969.

Bewitched. Season 6, episode 22. "Serena Stops the Show." Written by Richard Baer. Directed by Richard Michaels. Sony Pictures, February 1970.

Bewitched. Season 6, episode 26. "Chance on Love." Written by John L. Greene. Directed by Richard Michaels. Sony Pictures, March 1970.

Bewitched. Season 7, episode 4. "Samantha's Hot Bedwarmer." Written by Ed Jurist. Directed by William Asher. Sony Pictures, October 1970.

Bewitched. Season 7, episode 5. "Darrin on a Pedestal." Written by Bernie Kahn. Directed by William Asher. Sony Pictures, October 1970.

Bewitched. Season 7, episode 11. "The Corsican Cousins." Written by Ed Jurist. Directed by Richard Michaels. Sony Pictures, December 1970.

Bewitched. Season 7, episode 17. "The Return of Darrin the Bold." Written by Ed Jurist. Directed by Richard Michaels. Sony Pictures, February 1971.

Bewitched. Season 7, episode 19. "Samantha and the Troll." Written by Lila Garrett and Joel Rapp. Directed by William Asher. Sony Pictures, February 1971.

Bewitched. Season 7, episode 21. "Mixed Doubles." Written by Richard Baer. Directed by William Asher. Sony Pictures, March 1971.

Bewitched. Season 7, episode 22. "Darrin Goes Ape." Written by Leo and Pauline Townsend. Directed by Richard Michaels. Sony Pictures, March 1971.

Bewitched. Season 7, episode 25. "Samantha's Psychic Slip." Written by John L. Greene. Directed by William Asher. Sony Pictures, April 1971.

Bewitched. Season 8, episode 17. "Serena's Richcraft." Written by Michael Morris. Directed by William Asher. Sony Pictures, January 1972.

Bewitched. Season 8, episode 19. "Serena's Youth Pill." Written by Michael Morris. Directed by E.W. Swackhamer. Sony Pictures, February 1972.

Bonanza. Season 4, episode 27. "Mirror of a Man." Written by A.I. Bezzerides. Directed by Lewis Allen. National Broadcasting Company, March 1963.

The Brady Bunch. Season 3, episode 20. "Sergeant Emma." Written by Harry Winkler. Directed by Jack Arnold. American Broadcasting Company, 1972.

Bullock, Katharine. "Orientalism on Television: A Case Study of *I Dream of Jeannie*." *ReOrient*, 10/2018, Volume 4, Issue 1.

Cantor, Paul A. *Gilligan Unbound: Pop Culture in the Age of Globalization*. Lanham, MD: Rowman & Littlefield, 2002.

The Dark Mirror. Directed by Robert Siodmak. Written by Nunnally Johnson (screenplay) and Vladimir Pozner (story). Starring Olivia de Havilland. Nunally Johnson Productions, 1946.

Dead Ringer. Directed by Paul Henreid. Written by Albert Beich (screenplay), Oscar Millard (screenplay), and Rian James (story). Starring Bette Davis. Warner Bros., 1964.

Doane, Mary Ann. *Femmes Fatales: Feminism, Film Theory, Psychoanalysis*. New York: Routledge, 1991.

Doctor Who. Season 7, episodes 19-25. "Inferno." Written by Dennis Spooner. Directed by Christopher Barry. BBC Network, 1965.

Double Indemnity. Directed by Billy Wilder. Written by Billy Wilder and Raymond Chandler. Paramount Picture, 1944.

Douglas, Susan J. *Where the Girls Are: Growing Up Female with the Mass Media*. New York: Three Rivers Press, 1995.

Duke, Patty. *Call Me Anna: The Autobiography of Patty Duke*. New York: Bantam Books, 1987.

Eden, Barbara. *Jeannie, Out of the Bottle*. New York: Three Rivers Press, 2011.

The Feminist and the Fuzz. Directed by Jerry Paris. Written by James Henerson. Starring Barbara Eden. Screen Gems, January 1971.

Friedan, Betty. *The Feminine Mystique*. Tenth Anniversary Edition. New York: W.W. Norton & Company, Inc., 1974.

———. "Television and *The Feminine Mystique*." *American Decades Primary Sources*. Ed. Cynthia Rose, vol. 7.

Friends. Season 1, episodes 16-17. "The One with Two Parts." Written by David Crane and Marta Kaufman. Directed by Michael Lembeck. Warner Bros., February 1995.

Friends. Season 2, episode 10. "The One with Russ." Written by Ira Ungerleider. Directed by Thomas Schlamme. Warner Bros., January 1996.

Get Smart. Season 5, episode 21. "And Only Two Ninety-Nine." Written by Arne Sultan. Directed by Don Adams. CBS Network, February 1970.

Gilligan's Island. "All About Eva." Gilligan's Island. Writ. Joanna Lee. Dir. Jerry Hopper. CBS Network, 1966.

Gilligan's Island. "Gilligan vs. Gilligan." Writ. Joanna Lee. Dir. Jerry Hopper. CBS Network, 1966.

Hall, Stuart, ed., *Representation: Cultural Representations and Signifying Practices*. London: Sage, 1997.

Humphreys, Kristi Rowan. *Housework and Gender in American Television: Coming Clean*. Lanham, MD: Lexington Books, 2017.

———. "Supernatural Housework" *Home Sweat Home*. Elizabeth Patton and Mimi Choi, eds. Lanham, MD: Rowman and Littlefield, 2014.

I Dream of Jeannie. Season 1, episode 5. "G. I. Jeannie." Written by Bill Davenport. Directed by Alan Rafkin. Screen Gems, October 1965.

I Dream of Jeannie. Season 1, episode 4. "Jeannie and the Marriage Caper." Written by Tom Waldman and Frank Waldman. Screen Gems, October 1965.

I Dream of Jeannie. Season 1, episode 8. "The Americanization of Jeannie." Written by Arnold Horwitt. Directed by Gene Nelson. Screen Gems, November, 1965.

I Dream of Jeannie. Season 1, episode 9. "Moving Finger." Written by Harry Essex and Jerry Seelan. Directed by Gene Nelson. Screen Gems, October 1965.

I Dream of Jeannie. Season 3, episode 3. "Jeannie or the Tiger," Written by James Henerson. Directed by Hal Cooper. Screen Gems, September 1967.

I Dream of Jeannie. Season 3, episode 18. "Genie, Genie, Who's Got the Genie?" Written by James Henerson. Directed by Hal Cooper. Screen Gems, January 1968.

I Dream of Jeannie. Season 3, episode 24. "Have You Ever Had a Genie Hate You?" Written by Allan Devon. Directed by Claudio Guzman. Screen Gems, March 1968.

I Dream of Jeannie. Season 3, episode 25. "Operation: First Couple on the Moon." Written by Arthur Julian. Directed by Claudio Guzman. Screen Gems, March 1968.

I Dream of Jeannie. Season 4, episode 10. "How to Marry an Astronaut." Written by James Henerson. Directed by Hal Cooper. Screen Gems, December 1968.

I Dream of Jeannie. Season 4, episode 24. "Jeannie-Go-Round." Written by James Henerson. Directed by Claudio Guzman. Screen Gems, April 1969.

I Dream of Jeannie. Season 5, episode 12. "My Sister, the Home Wrecker." Written by James Henerson. Directed by Claudio Guzman. Screen Gems, December 1969.

I Married a Witch. Written by Robert Pirosh and Marc Connelly (screenplay). Directed by René Clair. Starring Veronica Lake. Paramount Pictures, 1942.

Knight Rider. Season 2, episodes 1–2. "Goliath." Written by Glen A. Larson. Directed by Winrich Kolbe. Glen A. Larson Productions, October 1983.

Kornfield, Sarah. "The E-man-ci-pation of Jeannie: Feminist Doppelgangers on U.S. Television." *Communication, Culture & Critique*.

Leibman, Nina C. *Living Room Lectures: The Fifties Family in Film and Television*. Austin, TX: University of Texas Press, 1995.

Lowe, Denise. *Women and American Television: An Encyclopedia*. Santa Barbara: ABC-Clio, 1999.

Luckett, Moya. "Girl Watchers: Patty Duke and Teen TV." *The Revolution Wasn't Televised: Sixties Television and Social Conflict*. Lynn Spigel and Michael Curtin, eds. New York: Routledge, 1997.

Marc, David. *Comic Visions: Television Comedy and American Culture*. Boston: Unwin Hyman, 1989.

The Marvelous Mrs. Maisel. Created, directed, and written by Amy Sherman-Palladino. Starring Rachel Brosnahan. Amazon Original, 2017.

Metz, Walter. *Bewitched*. Detroit: Wayne State UP, 2007.

O'Neill, William L. *Coming Apart: An Informal History of the 1960s*. New York: Times Books, 1971.

The Patty Duke Show. Season 1, episode 3. "The Elopement." Written by Sheldon. Directed by Asher. United Artists, October 1963.

The Patty Duke Show. Season 1, episode 4. "The House Guest." Written by Sheldon. Directed by Asher. United Artists, October 1963.

The Patty Duke Show. Season 1, episode 5. "The Birds and the Bees Bit." Written by Sidney Sheldon. Directed by Stanley Prager. United Artists, October 1963.

The Patty Duke Show. Season 1, episode 6. "Slumber Party." Written by Pauline and Leo Townsend. Directed by Stanley Prager. United Artists, October 1963.

The Patty Duke Show. Season 1, episode 7. "The Babysitters." Written by R.S. Allen. Directed by Stanley Prager. United Artists, October 1963.

The Patty Duke Show. Season 1, episode 8. "The Conquering Hero." Written by Jerry David and Lee Loeb. Directed by Asher. United Artists, November 1963.

The Patty Duke Show. Season 1, episode 9. "The President." Written by Sydney Sheldon. Directed by Stanley Prager. United Artists, November 1963.

The Patty Duke Show. Season 1, episode 10. "Double Date." Written by Rick Singer and Dick Chevillat. Directed by Stanley Prager. United Artists, November 1963.

The Patty Duke Show. Season 1, episode 11. "The Actress." Written by Sydney Sheldon. Directed by Stanley Prager. United Artists, November1963.

The Patty Duke Show. Season 1, episode 12. "How to Be Popular." Written by Sydney Sheldon. Directed by William Asher. United Artists, December 1963.

The Patty Duke Show. Season 1, episode 13. "The Songwriters." Written by Sydney Sheldon. Directed by William Asher. United Artists, December 1963.

The Patty Duke Show. Season 1, episode 14. "The Princess Cathy." Written by Sydney Sheldon. Directed by Stanley Prager. United Artists, December 1963.

The Patty Duke Show. Season 1, episode 17. "Horoscope." Written by Sydney Sheldon. Directed by Alan Rafkin. United Artists, January 1964.

The Patty Duke Show. Season 1, episode 18. "The Tycoons." Written by Sydney Sheldon. Directed by Alan Rafkin. United Artists, January 1964.

The Patty Duke Show. Season 1, episode 23. "Are Mothers People." Written by Sidney Sheldon. Directed by Stanley Prager. United Artists, February 1964.

The Patty Duke Show. Season 1, episode 31. "Patty, the Foster Mother." Written by Sydney Sheldon. Directed by Stanley Prager. United Artists, April 1964.

The Patty Duke Show. Season 1, episode 34. "The Little Dictator." Written by Sydney Sheldon. Directed by Stanley Prager. United Artists, May 1964.

The Patty Duke Show. Season 1, episode 35. "The Working Girl." Written by Sydney Sheldon. Directed by Stanley Prager. United Artists, May 1964.

The Patty Duke Show. Season 2, episode 18. "The Perfect Hostess." Written by Arnold Horwitt. Directed by Don Weis. United Artists, January 1965.

Peters, Jenny. "The gentleman preferred a blonde." *Variety* February 20-26, 2006, B4.

Sabrina, The Teenage Witch. Season 3, episode 25. "The Good, the Bad and the Luau." Written by Jonathon Schmock and Nancy Cohen. Directed by Linda Day. Viacom Productions, May 1999.

Said, Edward. "Orientalism Reconsidered." *Cultural Critique*. Fall 1985.

Schwartz, Sherwood. *Inside Gilligan's Island: From Creation to Syndication*. Jefferson, NC: McFarland, 1988.

Seipp, Catherine. "Gilligan's Island vs the Taliban," *Reason.com,* October 10, 2001, http://reason.com/archives/2001/10/10/gilligans-island-vs-the-taliba.

Sheldon, Sydney. *The Other Side of Me*. New York: Warner Books, 2005.

Spigel, Lynn and Michael Curtin, eds. *The Revolution Wasn't Televised: Sixties Television and Social Conflict*. New York: Routledge, 1997.

Star Trek. Season 2, episode 4. "Mirror, Mirror." Written by Jerome Bixby. Directed by Marc Daniels. Desilu Productions, October 1967.

A Stolen Life. Directed by Curtis Bernhardt. Written by Catherine Turney (screenplay), Margaret Burnell Wilder (adaptation), and Karel J. Benes (book). Starring Bette Davis. Warner Bros., 1946.

Sunset Boulevard. Directed by Billy Wilder. Written by Charles Brackett, Billy Wilder, and D.M. Marshman Jr. Paramount Pictures, 1950.

Twins of Evil. Directed by John Hough. Written by Tudor Gates. Starring Peter Cushing. Hammer Productions, 1971.

Venom. Written by Jeff Pinker (screenplay and story), Scott Rosenberg (screenplay and story), and Kelly Marcel (screenplay). Directed by Ruben Fleischer. Starring Tom Hardy. Columbia Pictures, 2018.

Vertigo. Directed by Alfred Hitchcock. Written by Alec Coppel and Samuel A. Taylor (screenplay). Paramount Pictures, 1958.

Index

About the Author

Kristi Rowan Humphreys is a Lecturer in the Department of English at Baylor University. She specializes in gender media and popular culture studies, film musicals and musical theater, and the visual culture of novelist William Faulkner. Her first monograph, *Housework and Gender in American Television: Coming Clean*, examined representations of housework and their relationships with gender in sixty of the most popular television shows of the 1950s through the 1980s. Most importantly, she is a proud wife to Chris and mom to Rowan and Lawson. She hails from the small town of Lorena, Texas, where she was reared to love God, family, and those Baylor Bears.